PART I

Pain & Possibility

"We make changes when the pain of being the same is greater than the pain that comes with changing our behavior." We are motivated to change when we feel the pain of being the same.

—Henry Cloud

Movement is the essence of living. Think about it--we're homo sapiens. These feet and legs were developed over millions of years by humans to allow us to stand up and move around our daily lives. This is what we were designed to do. We ignore this fact, and instead take our systems as a given, sitting in constant, continuous sitting.

Americans spend an average of 13 hours sitting and 8 hours sleeping each night. This has led to a sedentary life of 21 hours per day. Despite Americans being aware of the importance exercise, only 31% go to the gym and 56% spend less than $10 per week to stay active.

Your life is movement and your movement determines your life. Think about it for a second. Imagine being able to pick up your child from wherever you are without any pain. You could even run your first 5K, half marathon. Maybe you can sleep for a whole night without experiencing back pain?

People who want to live a healthier, pain-free life have found that they need to be able to comprehend their bodies, provide guidance and maintain accountability. To help you achieve lasting results in your health and wellbeing journey, I am here to assist you. Let me tell you a little bit about my journey.

After graduating college, I began a career as a corporate financial manager. It was not a good fit. After that, I switched jobs to fulfill my innate purpose or to be who and what I truly wanted to feel, move and just be. I began to experience significant pain in my body that led to a variety of symptoms. I began to feel more ill, suffering from everything from shingles to pneumonia to fainting episodes. I retrained and corrected my mistakes to pursue a career as a health and wellness professional. I wanted autonomy, knowledge, as well as the ability to make a difference in people's lives. I discovered the intricacies and how to listen to my body. This helped me to help others and their journey to better health and wellbeing.

After completing my residency post-doctorate, I realized that education and empowerment of others was a key part of my work. People deserve to see results and that meant getting to the root cause of their problems. They required a sustainable, effective and efficient solution.

It was more proactive than reactive to improve your health and well-being. Movement was, and remains, the answer.

With greater clarity, I changed my mindset and created a business. Then, I practiced and modelled a new way to live. Motion Therapy is a business that shares pain relief and rewards people who make progress towards a pain-free life. It supports people who want to reduce the common imbalances caused by too much sitting.

Research shows that more movement is what we need, and not more standing. This illustration shows all the factors that contribute to excessive sitting. Poor respiration, organ damage and muscle degeneration are all offset by movement.

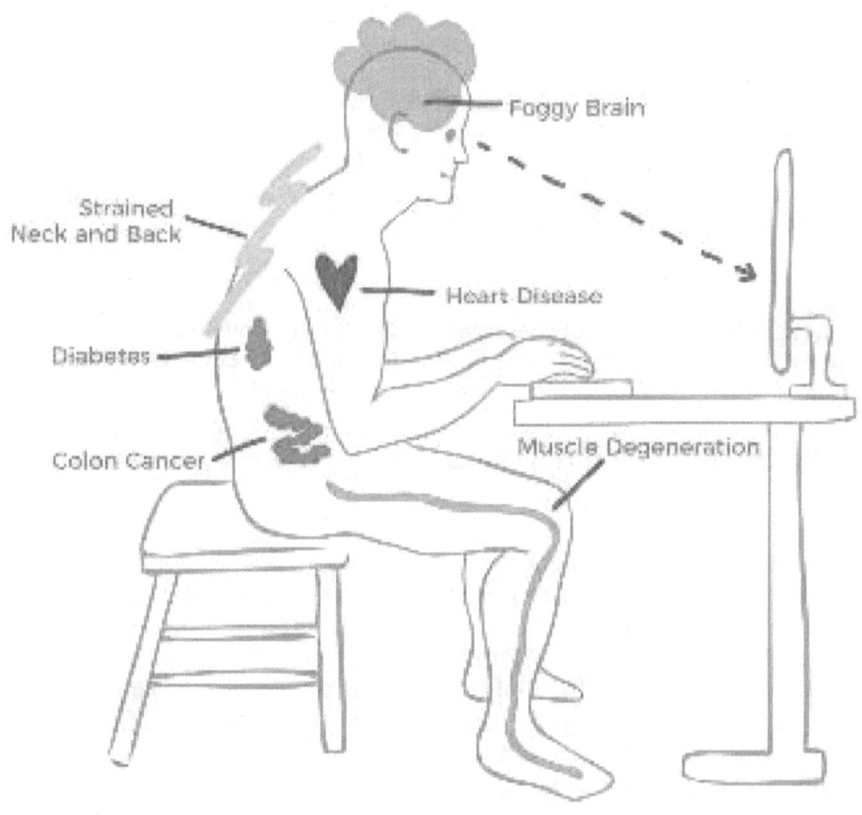

You are reading this book because something is calling you or urging you to live an active lifestyle. The truth about sedentary living is here for you. You can feel energized, no matter where or what you do. I'm your guide and you will learn the proven techniques and tools.

Chapter 1: Unpack Your Pain

"Trust yourself. You can be the person you want to live with for the rest of your life.

—Golda Meir

Understanding your pain and your possibilities is the key to your success in your health and well-being journey. Many people are looking for a quick fix. They want instant relief and immediate relief from all their aches and pains. Yes, I do. Your success may not come quickly, but it doesn't take a complex or time-consuming approach.

Amy's hip tightness and low back pain were reasons Amy first came to me not too long ago. Amy is a late-thirties independent business owner who is creative and innovative in both her personal life and her professional life. Her story revealed that her pain prevented her from being able to sit comfortably while she drove and worked on her laptop.

Amy had been to several health-care professionals, but her symptoms were not completely resolved. It was difficult for her to maintain her home exercise routine. She learned to be accountable by integrating the 10-Minute Fitness Maintenance System (chapter 7), into her workday. This was achieved by making the 10-Minute Body Maintenance System a daily habit and practicing her stretches and exercises every day. She moved from having to see a host of providers with different opinions about what she should do, to no longer needing them. It was a wonderful feeling to see her become pain-free. All my clients should not have to see me. This means that the solution works. It does.

Steven frequently travels internationally. He found that his neck, mid back, and shoulders bothered him during flights, commutes, as well as long hours in the office. The temporary solutions and the continued effort required were frustrating to Steven. He learned about proper alignment and regular movement, which helped him understand the root cause of his pain. It also taught him how to reduce risk and prevent future problems. He was able to change the behavior that was causing him pain by having this information and taking action. He lives pain-free today.

You can live a pain-free lifestyle. Understanding where you have been is the first step to understanding where you want to go. Then, you can use the same tools and techniques that Amy and Steven. Let's get started.

What would you say about your current situation? Consider what is happening to your body. Are you feeling tightness in your neck and upper back? Is there tingling or numbness in your left arm? Low back pain?

It doesn't matter what's happening, it is important to use adjectives to describe what's going on. Describe the sensation and its location. Consider the factors that can aggravate or alleviate your symptoms.

Use these specific adjectives to describe your symptoms or pain. Is it dull, sharp, throbbing or numbing? Are you stinging intermittently or constantly?

My current condition:

Where I feel it:

How it feels:

Your symptoms can be rated on a scale from 1-10 (1 = no pain to 10 = extreme pain):

1 2 3 4 5 6 7 8 9 10

When I do this activity, I feel my symptoms change:

How do you define your functional limitations? Consider how your pain, symptoms, or limitations prevent you from performing daily activities. Maybe your left arm is too low to lift above your head or your head feels stuck when driving. Maybe you have knee pain and can't run as fast as you want. What are your functional limitations and what do you need to do? What activities seem impossible? These areas restrict my body's movement:

How is your condition evolving? Dive a little deeper, going back into your past. You can recall when the pain started and when it ended. You should also consider the times when the pain, condition, or symptoms have changed, improved, or worsened. What was the situation? What could you have done differently? Which major life events, if any are still happening in your life?

Perhaps your low back pain started 20 years ago after an injury, but has increased since you got a new job. It's only gotten worse each year since that new job. Maybe you purchased a new chair for work and found that your low back pain is getting worse every day.

Sometimes, the story of our condition isn't clear until we look at the plot and connect all the dots. You may notice repeated patterns or trigger events that have contributed to your pain. You may have a short or longer story. You can move your story from your head to the pages of this guidebook. When we can connect our heads to our hearts and our bodies, powerful insights will emerge.

Consider the date at which the pain began, as well as any other incidents, injuries or key changes that may have occurred in your life.

My condition has a story. It's like this:

Physical Body Scan

Do a body scan if you are having trouble deciding what story to tell or if you want to find a powerful tool to identify pain, it is worth a quick scan.

Be still, seated or standing, for at least a minute. Ask and notice:

What am I feeling?
It's where are you feeling it?

How would you rate the pain on a scale from 1-10?

Although it takes only a few minutes, this technique can be extremely powerful. This technique allows you to become more aware of yourself, which leads to greater insight. You will gain clarity and notice any imbalances in your body through new insights. This information will give you clues about the next steps.

Before we move on to the specific exercises or techniques to manage pain, let's first examine why you want pain-free living.

Chapter 2: Know How You Want to Feel

"Knowing what you really want is the best form of clarity you can get.". This is the most creative and powerful thing you can do for your life.

--Danielle LaPorte - The Desire Map

When creating a client's health and wellness plan, there are some very important questions I ask. The first is "What's your vision?" Without a clear vision, clients will struggle to set goals.

It is essential to have a clear vision about the bigger, more general goal of your life. This will help you to see where you want to end up. This vision must be clear in your mind. You should also have an idea of how it will look physically. You must also determine how that vision makes you feel.

My client Ben is passionate about adventure travel. He has created his business to allow him to be independent from the location. He is determined to be healthy and fit to take on whatever adventure life throws at him. He had a simple vision: To be strong, confident, injury-free and strong, despite long hours running his business so that he is ready for any opportunity.

What's your vision?

As you work every day to realize your vision, it is the thing you will keep in mind. If you find yourself in doubt, fear, or indecision about the goal you have set, you can refer back to your vision and see if what you are doing is aligned with that vision. If it doesn't, that goal will not get you to where you want to go.

This handy litmus test is based on your vision. It is the reason you should do what you are doing. Your vision is the motivating, inspiring destination that you have purposely created. It is the large, expansive, and exciting picture of your future.

Vision is more than a wishful thinking. It is tied to the goals and actions that you take. This is your journey and your lifelong practice.

Next, ask this question after you have written down your vision:

What do you desire to feel in your body and mind?

Good, I'm sure! However, defining how you want to feel inside your body will be the bridge that connects your pain with your potential.

Danielle LaPorte explains in The Desire Map that identifying and describing your core desires is about understanding how you want to feel. It's also about recognizing the power of creating goals with your soul. Clarity comes from understanding how you want it to feel. This is part of a creative process that allows you to determine what you actually need in your life.

What do you desire to feel in your body and mind? Please be specific. Are you looking to feel confident? Vibrant? Beautiful? Stable? Flexible? Strong? Energized? Invincible? Lean? Light? Pain-free? Informed? Inspired? Attractive?

These are your core emotions:

These feelings can be triggered by what activities?

We experience both internal and external limitations when we are unable to function normally or enjoy the activities we love without pain. It can be difficult to play sports with your children if you are hurt. If we are in enough pain, it can make us dependent on others to help us dress or get to the bathroom.

These limitations are not to be ignored. These limitations are not a reason to judge. Instead, think about what you want to be able do to feel your "core desire feelings."

Jill, for example, was like many parents and wanted to lose 10 lbs. She had to manage multiple priorities, including managing her household, starting an online business and losing baby weight. She desired to feel free in her body. She wanted to feel happy, healthy, and beautiful. Renewed.

It was a conscious choice to choose daily activities that make Jill feel happy, beautiful, and energized. This led to some significant changes. She started yoga. She began a walking program. She also implemented the 10-Minute Body Management System into her lunchtime routine. It is crucial to incorporate routine body maintenance habits like Jill's into your daily life in order to achieve your desired feelings and ultimately your vision.

This is where you can commit to body maintenance that will support your feelings of happiness and well-being. Start with the three most important activities for you, even if there are others.

These are the activities I would like to do:

You are what you truly desire. It is the motivator that will enable you to develop body maintenance habits, reach your goals, and move towards your dreams.

Chapter 3: Use Your Vision to Create Your Goals

It doesn't matter how long it takes to get there, the point is to arrive at a destination.

—Eudora Welty

It is important to discuss your goals before you take the next step. Your goals are concrete, achievable outcomes you can plan for that will help you reach your vision. They are more than just wishes or hopes. They are concrete steps that will lead you to a life of value. With each success, they bring you closer to your vision.

Your goals are the waypoints on your road map, the places you want to go as you work towards your ultimate destination. Your vision should be aligned with your goals. You will need to have both short-term and long-term goals if you want to move beyond a state where you are in pain.

Small successes can create momentum and help you reach your short-term goals. If you have had major knee surgery, your short-term goals might be to get out of bed, use the bathroom unassisted, or move around the room. It may be possible to set a timer that reminds you to get up every hour for 10 minutes if you are experiencing back pain at work.

Your ultimate goal is to achieve your long-term goals. These could include the incorporation of the 10-Minute Body Management System into your daily life, and eventually becoming a part of your everyday routine. They may also include getting rid of the desk and setting up an active workspace (see chapter 6). Each long-term goal becomes a part of your daily life as you achieve it.

Write Down Your SMART Goals

These are two key rules to remember when setting goals. First, write down any goals that you have set. Writing down a goal is the most important factor in determining its success. Second, ensure that your goals are SMART goals. These are specific, measurable, achievable, realistic, time-bound, and attainable goals.

A SMART goal is one that's . . .

Specific: More is not better. Standing is more precise. Standing at your desk is more precise.

Measurable: It is important to be able track your progress towards your goals. You can track your daily progress by tracking things like "I will be standing three hours more per day", for example. It is easy to measure the success or failure of this endeavor.

Attainable: Some people might think that "I will stand every single day for five hours" is a lofty goal. It's possible to keep it achievable by saying, "I will stand for 30 minutes every hour between 9:00 a.m. - 3:00 p.m."

Realistic. You need to make sure that the goal is achievable and fits in your current life. It can be difficult to establish new habits during major life events. It is unlikely that you can start a rigorous exercise program when you are 28 weeks pregnant.

Time-bound. You should give your goal an end date so that you can measure its success and then check it. You may need to reset or extend the timeframe at that point. However, a goal without an end date will lead to poor results and lose momentum.

These are the guidelines:

"I'm going get up and move more" does not qualify as SMART.

"I will stand at my desk for three hours more per day, five times per week over the next two months," is a SMART goal.

Here are your short-term goals for health and well-being:

Here are your long-term wellness and health goals:

Compare these goals to your feelings and vision. Does this vision align with these goals? Are the listed goals likely to bring you the emotions you want? If yes, then I bet you have chosen the best goals in your life, your time, and your real world.

These goals will guide you as you move to Part II. Here you'll implement the system, tools and techniques that will help you on your journey to health and well-being.

PART II Tools & Techniques

"Transformation literally refers to going beyond your body." --Wayne Dyer

I know you feel overwhelmed after reading Part I and performing the exercises. It's okay. It's actually a sign that you have found some core truths about yourself, your desired feelings, and your SMART goals.

Believe in yourself. Let's then move on to what is undeniably at the heart of this guide, the techniques, strategies, and tools that will help you transform your pain into the realizations of your potential while you work. This is your Roadmap to Recover that will help you see that transformation.

Motion Therapy Roadmap to Recovery

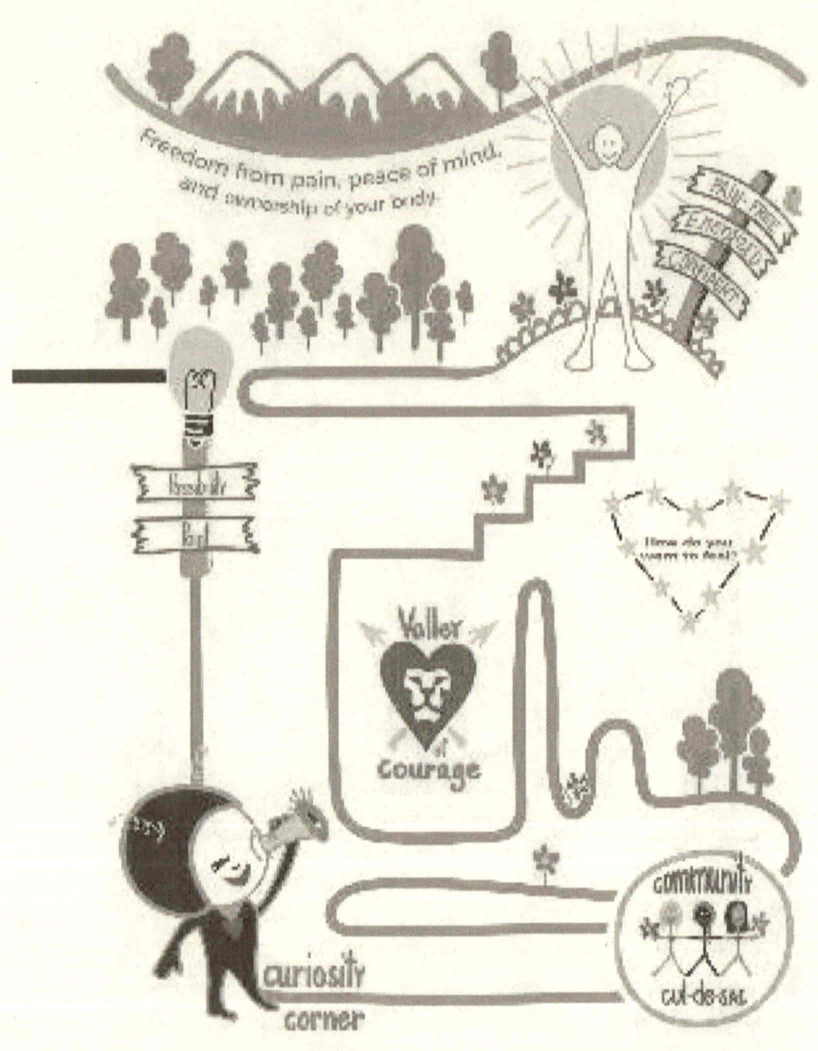

Freedom from pain, peace of mind,
and ownership of your body.
How do you
want to feel?
Valley
of
Courage
community
cul-de-sac
curiosity
corner

Part II teaches you how to avoid and eliminate pain from sitting too long:

- Techniques to Inspire "Shift"Tools: Active Workstation Design & Body MaintenanceStrategy: The 10-Minute Body Maintenance SystemThese strategies, tools, and techniques will help you live pain-free.

Chapter 4: Alignment, Posture, and the Root Cause Your Pain

"It was through the alignment and the body that my mind, self and intelligence were discovered." -- B.K.S. Iyengar

The Root Cause of Your Pain

Working with clients, I have found that the most painful, troubling, and common imbalances in the body are caused by a sedentary lifestyle. Sitting Disease is a result of a sedentary lifestyle. This includes too much sitting at the computer, desk job, or in a chair. Many people don't know that excessive sitting can cause aches and pains from the head to the toes and common imbalances to the root cause. Poor posture is the root of all this.

Active Workstation

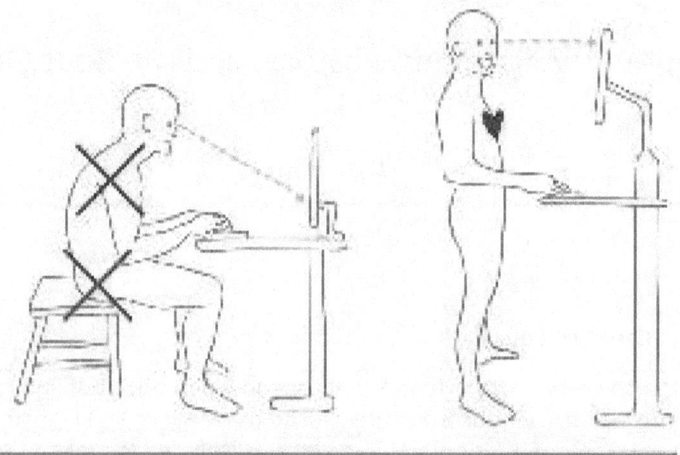

How we live, work and play is influenced by our posture. My clients have been more educated about proper posture than any other topic.

Look at the illustration's standing and sitting figures. When most people see the figure to the left, "bad posture" is the first thing that comes to mind. However, "good posture" is what most people associate with the figure to the right.

Postural imbalances can appear in many places and ways depending on who they are. As you can see, poor posture and alignment are the main causes of muscular imbalances known as Upper Crossed Syndrome or Lower Crossed Syndrome. This illustration shows the red X's. The red X's signify that the opposite group of weak and tight muscles is the source of imbalance.

Upper + Lower Crossed Syndromes

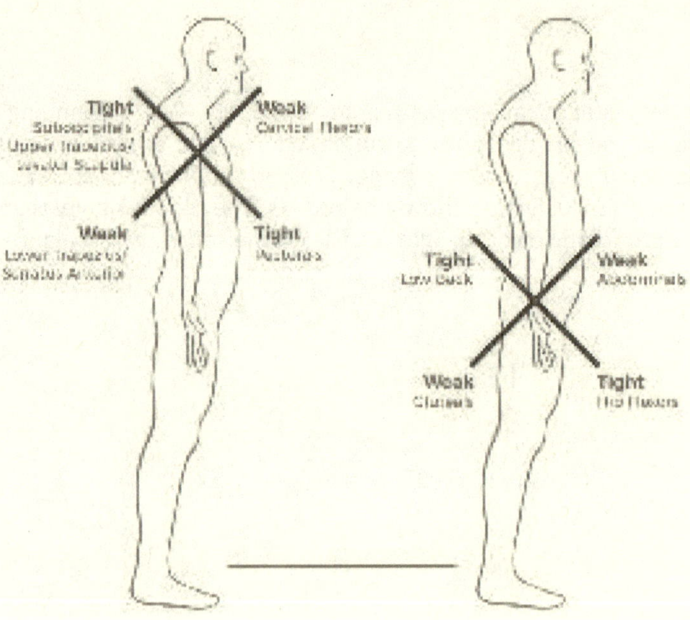

Upper Crossed Syndrome

Lower Crossed Syndrome

Upper Crossed Syndrome is characterized by imbalances in the upper body. This includes the neck, shoulders and upper back.

These imbalances can lead to forward heads, round shoulders, and a hunched upper back if the pectoral and upper trapezius muscles become too tight.

Lower Crossed Syndrome is characterized by imbalances in the pelvis, hip, low back, hip and abdominal regions.

These imbalances can lead to a forward belly, a curved lower spine and jammed hips.

These imbalances are caused by too much sitting. This can lead to muscle dysfunction, pain and injury.

Proper Posture Reflects Proper Alignment

So why is proper posture so important? A properly aligned body will show through proper posture. The best way to get everything moving is by aligning your body correctly. Your "system" will perform optimally if all 640 muscles are aligned and all 206 bones are in the right place. You can then do activities efficiently and effectively without any pain or limitation. It is simply how our bodies were designed.

Alignment is all about what's connected. Posture refers to what is seen.

<u>Alignment can be dynamic. Your body will align as it was designed to. You'll feel confident and calm throughout your day. You'll activate the same</u>

muscles people spend thousands of dollars on "core training" and hours in the gym to develop.

Static posture is what you are. It is essentially a snapshot showing how your body looks at any given time. Your posture changes constantly because you are an active, breathing, living human being. As you live a dynamic, active lifestyle, at work and at home, we focus on alignment rather than posture.

No matter how you are sitting or standing, the goal is to achieve optimal alignment. This is a key factor in managing imbalances and eliminating the pain symptoms of Upper or Lower Crossed Syndromes.

Now that you know the importance of alignment in your daily life, it is time to focus on how your breath helps you maintain a healthy, natural alignment.

Chapter 5: Breathe and Mindful Building of Your Core

"It is important to not stop asking questions. "Curiosity has its own reason to exist."

—Einstein

As we have discussed, Sitting Disease can eventually lead to whole-body dysfunction in varying degrees. It can ultimately be fatal to the mind, body, and spirit. It is possible to prevent it and many people are able to reverse it. How?

Start by becoming more aware, knowledgeable, and proactive, focusing on your sitting habits. Spend at least one day observing how much time you spend sitting down. These "Sitting Stats", which are a snapshot of how long you spend sitting still versus living a more active lifestyle, will give you an idea of your daily activity. This powerful tool will help you gain a better understanding of your sedentary habits. This tool will help you understand your risk of developing Sitting Disease.

My Sitting Stats:

It is powerful to assess how much time we sit in our day to day life. Use this self-assessment tool to keep track of your sedentary hours in one 24-hour period.

Eat Breakfast ______ Hours

Commute to Work ______ Hours

Work in the Morning ______ Hours

Eat Lunch ______ Hours

Work in the Afternoon ______ Hours

Commute Home ______ Hours

Eat Dinner ______ Hours

Relax/Leisure ______ Hours

Other ______ Hours

Total Sitting Time- ______ Hours

When you review your "Sitting Stats", don't be surprised if you find that you are sitting a lot. "More that half of the average person's waking hours are spent sitting, whether they're watching TV, working at a desk, driving, or engaging in other activities. [16] Chronic sitting is the main reason so many people experience unnecessary pain. This guidebook was created to help.

Many of us unconsciously have a habit of sitting for long periods of time. This is due to poor posture. When shallow breathing is practiced, oxygenated air tends not to circulate deep enough to reach the abdomen.

Core muscles can weaken if you don't practice deep, purposeful breathing. As mentioned, if your core muscles are weakened by poor posture and chronic sitting, you're more susceptible to developing Upper or Lower Crossed Syndrome.

Core Muscles

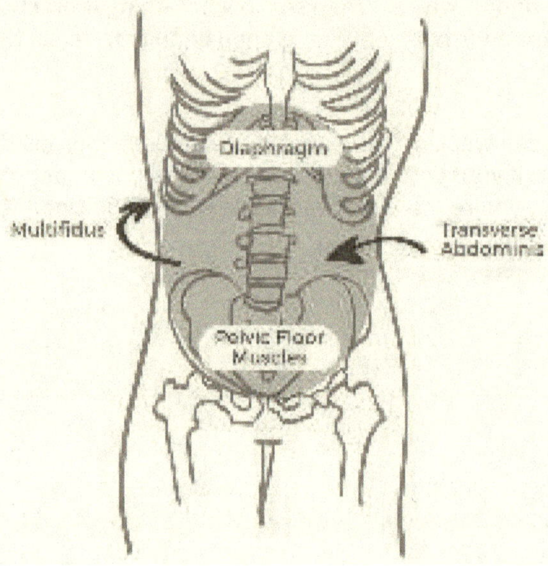

For pain-free living, breathing is one of the most important and overlooked tools. As breathing is the living thing, it can also be used to relieve stress and anxiety, improve digestion, increase immunity, promote physical comfort and overall well-being. Proactively engaging your breathing muscles in a natural, balanced way--that is, with mindful breathing--contributes to good alignment.

The next two images will help you prepare for your next action steps. The first illustrates how the breath connects to our core. The second illustration shows how balloon breathing can be used to improve your ability to inhale and strengthen the diaphragmatic muscles as well as the core. [17]

Your Breath + Core

Inhalation: When breathing in, your diaphragm contracts, moving air in and downward.

Exhalation: When breathing out, your diaphragm relaxes, moving air upward and out.

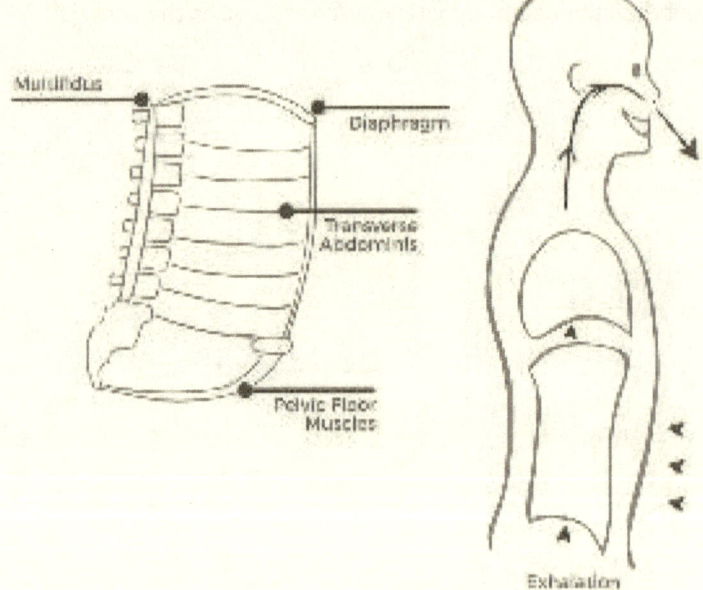

Breathing in (inhaling) causes your diaphragm to contract, moving oxygenated blood in and out of the chest cavity.

Breathing out (exhaling) causes your diaphragm to relax, moving carbon dioxide upwards through the chest cavity.

Your body will compensate for insufficient contraction and relaxation of your diaphragm to get air into other muscles. This can lead to imbalances that can often lead to pain. How do you breathe? Practice awareness. Next, become curious and observe how your breathing changes as you use the techniques below.

Balloon breathing is a way to improve your ability to inhale. This improves posture and fine-tunes neuromuscular control for 1) the transverse abdominis and 2) the diaphragm.

This illustration shows that when all of these muscles work together, it allows for optimal activity in your body. They protect us from everyday dangers.

To help you integrate the Postural Restoration Institute's(tm) exercise into your daily life, I have adopted it.

You can continue with the 10-Minute Body Care System.

This breathing technique (chapter 7) will be the cornerstone of your success.

Balloon Breathing Exercise

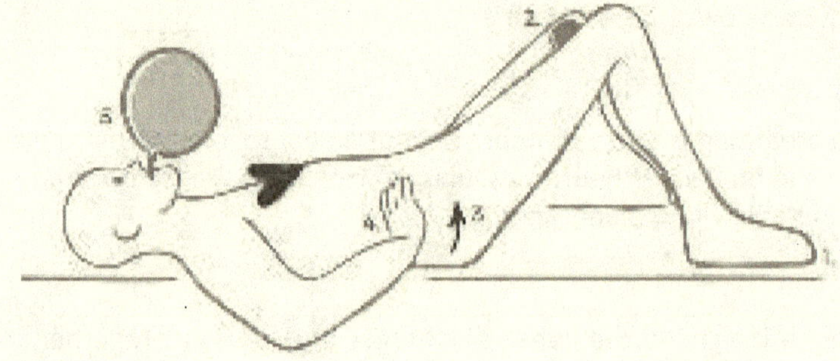

1. Body: Lay on your back, with your knees bent.Legs: Place a ball of 4-6 inches or a towel between your knees to engage your inner thigh muscles.Reverse the position and tilt your tailbone towards your belly. This posterior pelvic tilt should be maintained for the duration of the exercise.Place your hands on your lower abdomen.Core: Inhale through your nose and expand your belly. Exhale through your mouth and blow air into the balloon. (Use your imagination, if necessary). You should not let the balloon air out, but instead hold it in your nose and inhale through your nose to take in any remaining breaths.Relax your entire body and continue the inhale-exhale intoballoon cycle until the balloon is full.Try this exercise and see if your core muscles are engaged under your hands.It is often surprising to discover the power of breathing. This helps to increase awareness of the mind and body. Mindful breathing can also help to calm the mind, heart, and body in a highly integrated way.

There are many other forms of mindfulness that you can practice. These practices are not covered in this guidebook. However, you might consider other options, such as yoga or massage, or online resources and apps like Headspace(r), my personal favorite.

Andy Puddicombe of Headspace states that while we cannot change everything that happens in our lives, we can alter the way we experience it. This is the power of meditation and mindfulness. You don't need to light incense or sit down on the ground. You just need to take 10 minutes each day to pause and be present in the moment. This will help you feel more focused, calm, and clearer.

Mindful breathing can be a tool to help you become more aware of all aspects of your life. It's essential to the pain-free lifestyle and your journey. Your breath can help you be more patient with where you are, what you see, and how you feel. You can promote your body's natural movement to alleviate pain and balance by using or practicing the mindful breath techniques in this chapter.

As you perform the following exercises and stretching, you can bring your breathing to the forefront. This will help you create rhythm and maximize movement throughout your body.

Chapter 6: Grow Knowledge, Prepare to Move

"Efficiency concerns doing things right. Effectiveness is about doing the right thing." --Peter Drucker

We'll be using our breath work as a guideline in this chapter. These exercises and stretches are not easy to learn at first. It will take practice and careful integration into your daily routine.

As you make progress, you will feel empowered. You will feel empowered and able to reach your full potential. Your ability to think from the top and develop skills that will allow you to achieve long-lasting results. Each exercise creates a "shift," which is a shift in awareness of a sensation. This can be a release of tension, relief of pain, or greater mobility. This will help you feel more in control of your body.

Let's begin by looking at the importance of proper alignment techniques in creating positive change.

TECHNIQUES: Posture & Alignment to Invite "Shift"

To create pain-free motion in your life, you must first learn how to stand using what is called the "alignedstanding" technique. This simple technique will help you improve your standing alignment and adjust your whole body. This will also reduce the symptoms of Upper and Lower Crossed Syndromes.

You can now practice these five steps of aligned sitting wherever you are. During each step, remember to inhale through your nose and exhale through your mouth.

Aligned Standing Technique

Step 1: Neutral Pelvis

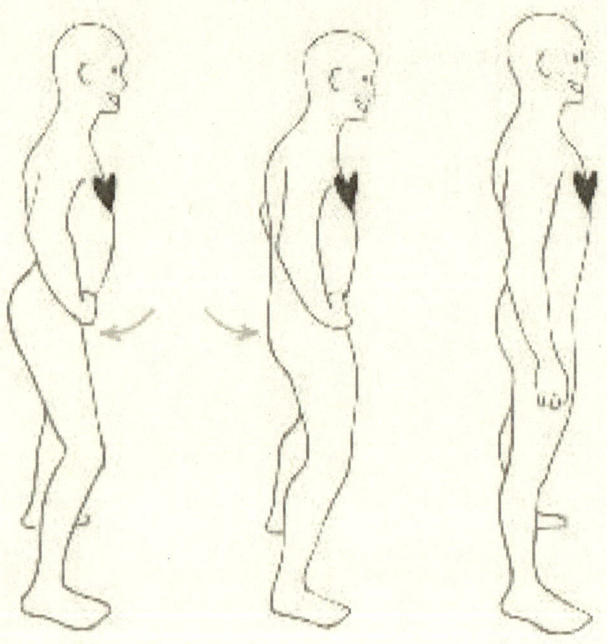

Step 1: Neutral Pelvis

1. Place your feet hip-width apart, and point your toes forward.Do not relax your knees.Your "neutral pelvis" is the place where your pelvis lies midway between being tilted forward or backward. To help you find your "neutral pelvis", place your hands on the hips and rock backward and forward six times. This will loosen the muscles around your pelvis, low back, hips, and pelvis. Be mindful to breathe.Find a comfortable place between the extremes of yourpelvis mobility.

Step 2: Spine Stacking

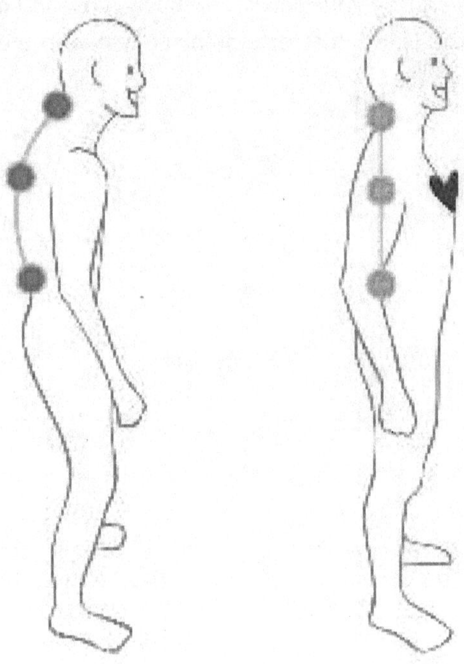

Step 2: Spine Stacking

As you align your spine to your neutral pelvis, think about stacking blocks. As tall, straight, and strong blocks, imagine them as such.

Step 3: Shoulder Reset

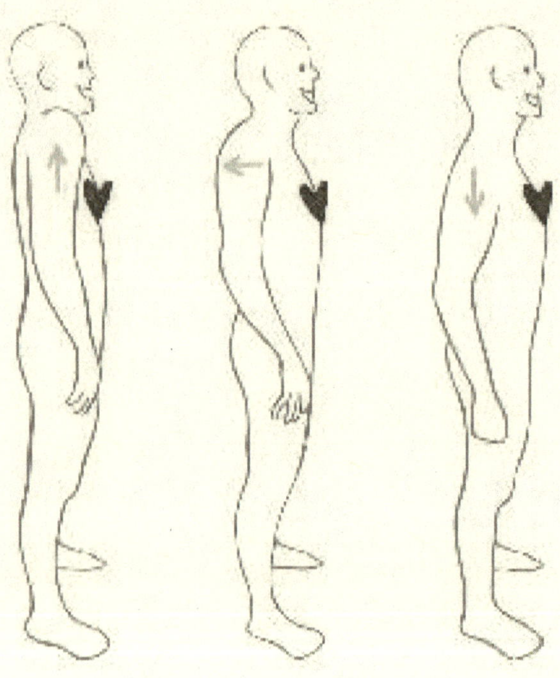

Step 3: Shoulder Reset

Your shoulders should be lifted towards your ears, then your shoulder blades should be rolled backwards.

Step 4: Chin Tuck

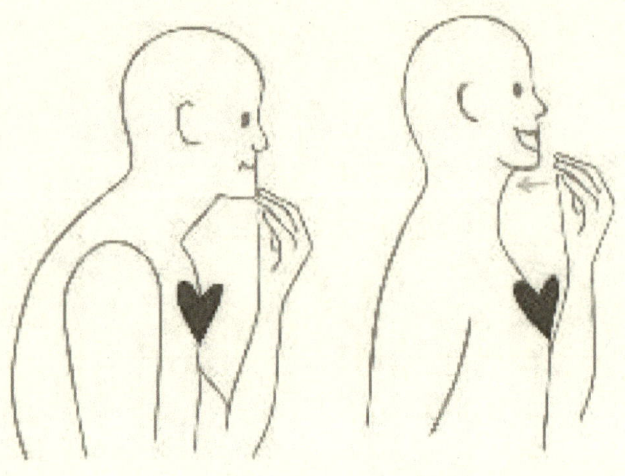

Step 4: Chin Tuck

Place one finger on each side of your chin. Your eyes should be looking forward. Then, gently move your head towards your hand until you feel some tension but no pain. This will align your neck, upper back and prevent a hunched-back position.

Step 5: Final Lift

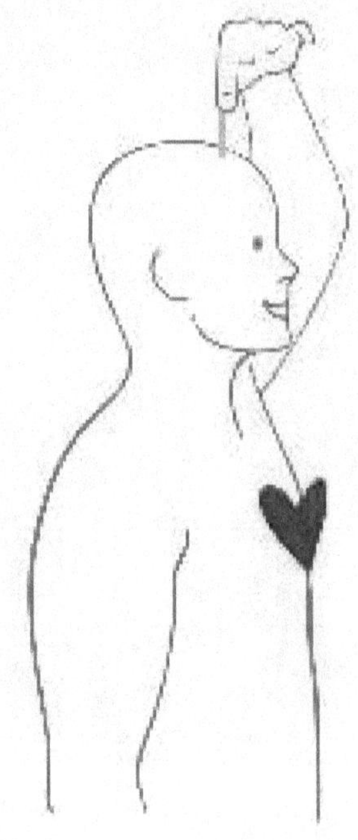

Step 5: Final Lift

Gently pull your crown hair toward the sky until your final lift.

It doesn't matter where or why you stand, it is important to check in with your body regularly. This aligned standing technique can be used to improve your real-world, real-life stance. You will feel more relaxed, energized and confident throughout your day.

Aligned Sitting Technique

Aligned sitting follows the same steps as aligned standing. Even though your lower half is "turned off," it is important to maintain head-to-hip alignment when you sit. Also, remember to keep your pelvis neutral.

Active Sitting

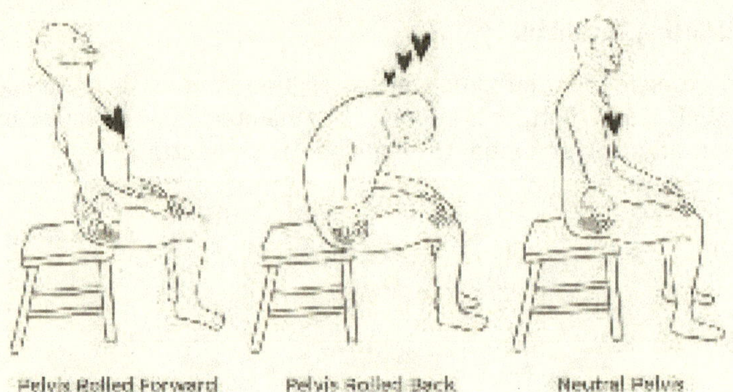

Place your feet flat on the ground and sit on the edge of the chair.

1. Your knees should be at 90 degrees or slightly below your hips.Place your hands on your thighs, and then roll your hips backward and forward.Your "neutral pelvis" is the place where your pelvis lies between being rotated forward and backward. To support yourself, incorporate your breath.Now that you are able to properly sit and stand, let's move on to the tools that will help you to improve your alignment skills.

TOOLS: Active Workstation Design

Active workstations are the space you create to maximize your body's performance and not reduce it. These workstations are also known as "sit-stand desks," "standing workstations," and "sit-stand stations." The goal of this guidebook is to create an active, pain-free lifestyle. This allows us to get out of our chairs and continue living our normal lives.

You may have noticed that sitting at your desk for long periods of time causes you to feel tired, sluggish and compressed in your spine. Your neck, shoulders, and hips feel tight. It is easy to find yourself moving around in your chair, trying to find a comfortable position. However, your body feels tense and confined at your desk. Although it doesn't feel like you have a disease, it can feel like you are suffering from dis-ease. It is possible to alleviate both the disease as well as the dis-ease by simply standing up and changing your position every 30 minutes. A daily body maintenance program can make a big difference!

Do you really need an adjustable, sit-stand desk or active workstation? To get rid of the Sitting Disease, can you simply make more trips to the water fountain or stand longer while talking on the phone? Yes, it is possible, but you are an ambitious and proactive hard worker who knows that small adjustments to your workday can have significant benefits over the course your entire life.

However, any movement is beneficial, but Mayo Clinic researchers found that participants who used a sit-stand desk to work on their study had a lower sedentary rate, burnt more calories and consumed less calories. This led to better health and productivity. [19]

You get direct benefits from the active workstation. It increases our activity level. It improves our mental, emotional, and physical health. Active workstations support better digestion and overall body function. It supports the body's basic needs, since we were designed to move.

It doesn't matter if you are sitting, standing, or leaning. Your alignment is important as you go about your day. Research has shown that alignment in sitting, standing, or leaning is vital for a healthy and active lifestyle. Lumo Bodytech Inc., the innovators of the technology-based posture coach, refers to this as "Your next posture is your best posture."

To put it another way, moving as much as you can is the best thing for your posture. Avoiding a static position for long periods of time is not a good idea. Most of us work at desks so it is important to learn how to stand and sit properly for our health. The human body was designed to move and not sit at a desk for 8 hours.[20]

According to Ohio State University's Spine Research Institute, upright leaning is an alternative to standing and sitting workstations. [21] The upright leaning option promotes balance, reduces spinal loads and lowers muscle forces. It can also be an important part of an ergonomic workstation design.

Active Workstation Design

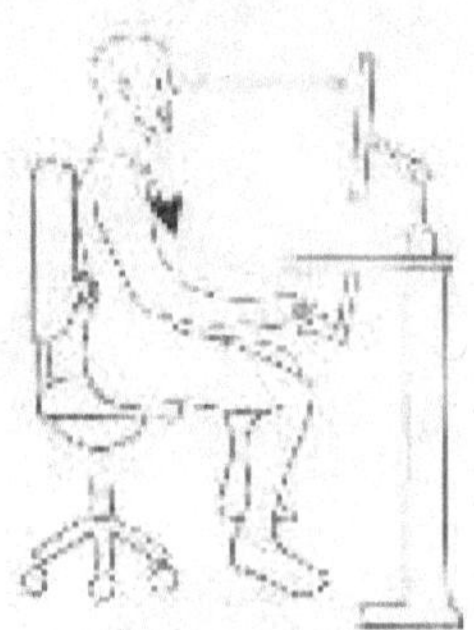

Sit Stand Desk

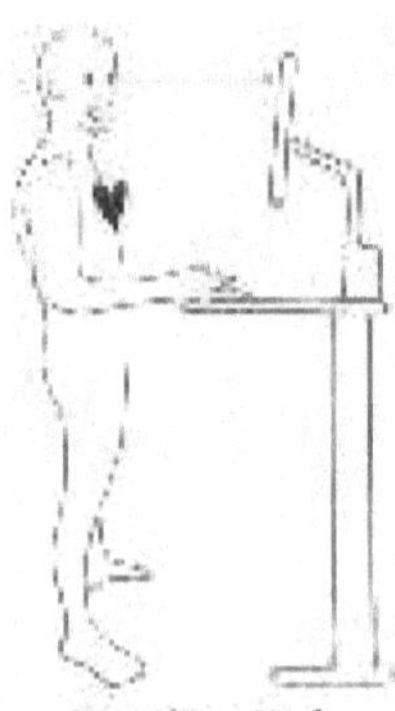

Standing Desk

Leaning Desk

There are many "tricks" that you can use to create an environment that supports your alignment. You can try DIY projects like using household items such as books or dictionaries to elevate your keyboard and keep your body aligned, engaged, and upright.

Here's a basic setup for an active workstation:

DIY Active Workstation Design

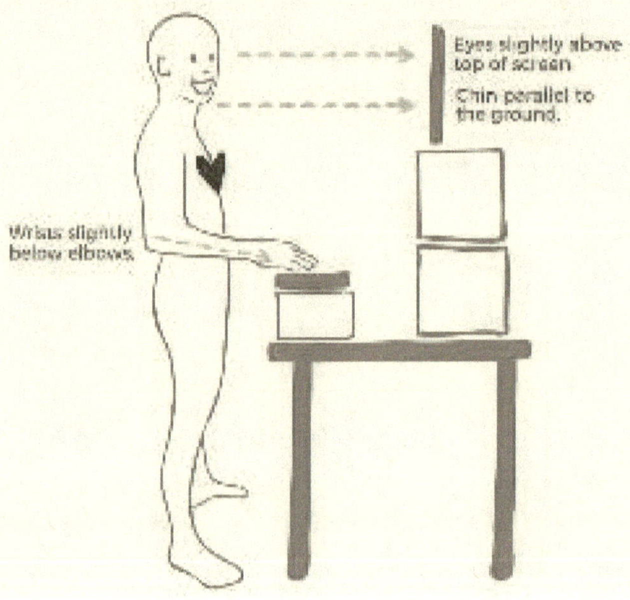

Checklist for DIY Active Workstation Design

- ✓ An adjustable laptop/monitor riser that allows you to place the monitor slightly below your eyes and is at arm's reachWireless keyboard
- ✓ Wireless mouse
- ✓ Support for keyboard and mouse at the wrist to keep neutral wristsAnti-fatigue mat
- ✓ Exercise ball or active seatSupportive footwear and foot restHeadset for phone use

It doesn't matter if you invest in an active desk or do it yourself, the goal is the same: to fit your body to your workspace, and not your body to the workstation.

Once you have created your active workspace, remember to pay attention to your body. This will help support your body's recovery and active alignment. Be aware of what your body needs in regards to your workstation layout and your standing goals. Make the necessary changes. For your ultimate standing goal, I recommend that you work up to standing for three hours more per day, five days per week.

You can take the time to evaluate what's working and what's not. This will help you to be curious and listen to your body, and make steady progress towards your goals. There are no rules. It's all about you, your preferences, and your ability.

TOOLS: Body Maintenance Tools

For the best results, regular body maintenance is essential to maintain the alignment and workstation design gains. Your muscles will need to be freed from knots and sore, painful areas of muscle fibers. These are commonly called trigger points. You can use some body maintenance tools to help. These tools will be integrated into the 10-Minute Body Maintain System.

Five tools are frequently recommended by me: Thera Cane and The Stick. Stretch Out is also a good option.

A foam roller, a strap, and a spiky balls are all good options. The best tool for you is the one that you choose. You should "try on" any tool that you are interested in. You don't have to buy the same tool as everyone else. A licensed health professional such as a physical therapist can provide a customized, more detailed prescription.

The spikyball is a self-massage device that can be carried around. It relieves tension in the hips and low back. The spiky ball can be carried in a backpack, purse, or suitcase. You only need a wall to help you relieve muscle pains.

The Theracane offers relief for the upper back, shoulders and neck.

Stick massages the lower back and legs. The Thera Cane, The Stick and the Spiky Ball are great tools for those who travel. These can be carried in your car, or you can store them in your travel bag.

Stretch Out Straps are for the lower body. They can be used to stretch the spine, low back, and feet. Foam rollers target the spine and mid back. They are also useful for "nerve gliding", which is a technique that helps soft tissue to move correctly and prevents related pain.

Body Maintenance Tools

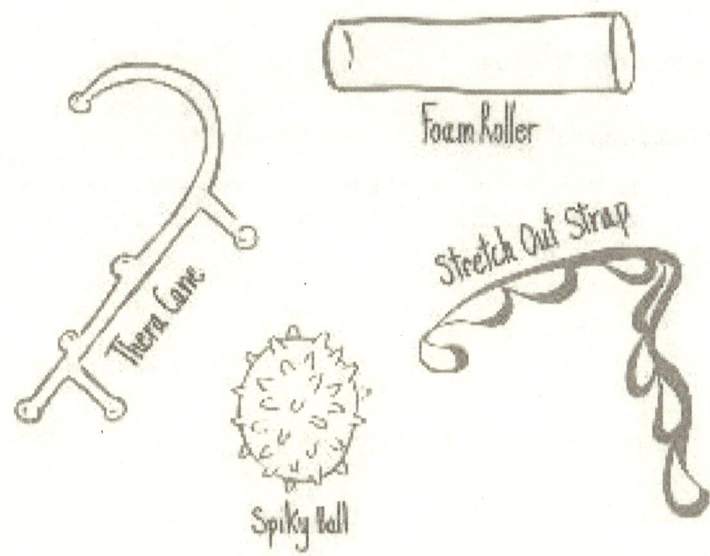

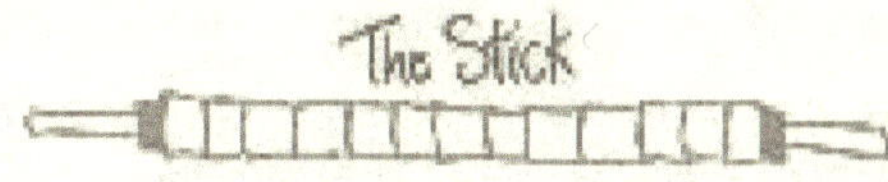

DIY Tip: Get creative!
Foam Roller = Rolled Yoga Mat or
Two Tennis Balls Taped Together
The Stick = Rolling Pin
Spiky Ball = Tennis Ball
Stretch Out Strap = Dog Leash

The following is a DIY tool for body maintenance:

Foam roller = A rolled yoga mat, or two tennis balls taped together

The Stick = rolling pin

Spiky tennis ball = Spiky Ball

Stretch Out Strap = dog leash

These body maintenance tools can be used to manage your symptoms. If your body is screaming for help, you can take action by choosing the tool that provides the best relief.

Trigger Points
+
Self-Massage Tools

Spiky Ball
Low Back & Hips

Thera Cane
Upper Back & Shoulders

The Stick
Legs & Low Back

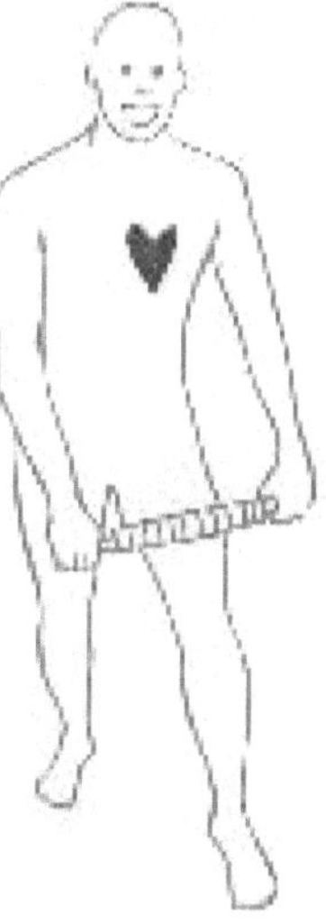

These tools also serve to remind you visually to take care of your body. You can practice them daily to help you develop your new lifestyle habits. These tools will remind you to act when an unpleasant, old feeling arises.

These are some maintenance exercises you can do with your Stretch Out Strap or foam roller. These exercises will allow you to release trapped nerves and muscles in your lower body, as well as tighten your joints.

Stretch Out Strap: Lower Body Nerve Glide

This exercise gently lengthens tight muscles and glides nerves. It also realigns spinal segments.

Stretch Out Strap
Lower Body Nerve Glide

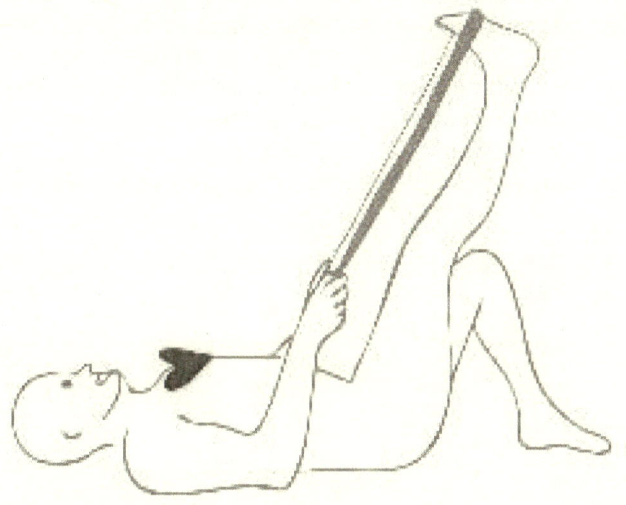

Body: Lay on your back, knees bent, feet on the ground.

1. Leg: Place a strap around your ankle and straighten your knee. Ensure that your ankle and knee are locked during this exercise.To release tension in your foot, gently lift your foot towards the sky. Next, let your foot go through the strap until it is loose enough to allow the tension to ease. Continue this 10 times, then switch sides.Begin to be curious. Breathe and discover your range of motion. Gently pull the strap towards or across your midline. How do you feel?Foam Roller: Mid Back Mobility

   Focus on the area around your mid back with the foam roller. The foam roller massages the back and mobilizes sections of the spine. Many of my clients describe the sensation of traction or elongation in their spines, which allows them to move more freely after prolonged periods of sitting.

Foam Roller: Mid Back Mobility

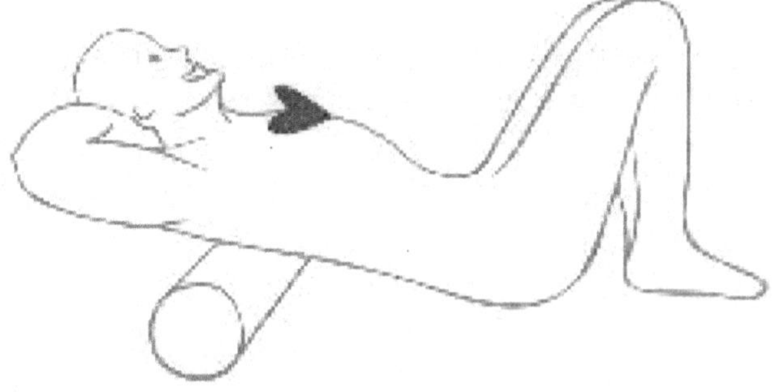

Body: Lay on your back, and then extend your mid-spine over the foam roller.

1. Hips + Knees - Bend your hips to the knees while keeping your hips and feet on the ground.To support your head, clasp your hands behind the neck.Take six deep breaths and gently stretch your spine across the foam roller. Every breath should help to relax tight muscles and stretch your mid back further over the foam roller. How do you feel?Foam Roller: Lower Body Mobility

   Now, roll your back, inner and outside thighs, and inner leg outwards. This will loosen tight muscles and relieve tension in the lower body.

   As you turn towards the ground, notice the slight twist in your upper body. As you go through the foam roller exercise, this rotation will increase your arm and core strength.

Foam Roller: Lower Body Mobility

Arms: Place your arms on the foam roller in the area of your symptoms.

1. Body: Use your body weight to apply sustainable pressure to your body. This will release trigger points and knots in the muscles.Take a moment to be curious. Roll your body weight onto and off the area of your symptoms. Notice what you feel?Now that you know the basics of how to relieve the pain from excessive sitting, let's look at how to incorporate them into the 10-Minute Body Maintenance Program.

Chapter 7: Power Up Your Practice

"Don't want it to be easier, wish it was better." --Jim Rohn

You should now have a solid knowledge of the techniques and tools you can use to get up from your chair, and not just sit there. Now you are ready to start the 10-Minute Body Maintenance Program.

What is a "system?" A system is essential for maintaining a pain-free and active lifestyle. The system includes 10 science-backed techniques to target imbalances caused by sitting for long periods of time. These exercises offer many benefits but we are using them to treat the most common imbalances that lead to Upper and Lower Crossed Syndromes. (See Part II at the beginning). These stretching techniques have been proven to be effective in relieving the symptoms of these syndromes. I have worked with individuals for over a decade.

It is easy to use and takes very little time. It doesn't require you to join a gym, buy weights, or sign-up for boot camp. You can simply move your body throughout the day and perform daily maintenance.

This system's convenience will allow you to stay consistent with your new active-lifestyle lifestyle habit.

You can also customize the system based on your feelings. The system is flexible enough that you don't need to do all exercises every day or use all of the tools. Once you have the system down, you can spend 10 minutes per day using the tool or technique that gives you the relief you seek.

STRATEGY: The 10-Minute Body Maintenance System

These 10 body maintenance exercises will target imbalances from head-to-toe. Start with the first technique and practice it for 10 minutes. Next, you should practice a different technique every day for 10 minutes. You'll be able to practice each of the 10 stretching methods after 10 days. Your body will be able to go through the initial run of the Head-to-Toe Body Maintenance System.

In your 10 minutes, you can also choose a body-maintenance tool to add to the daily exercise. As I mentioned in the previous chapter, I encourage clients to try each of the five tools to find the one that best addresses their pain. You can choose one of the three stretches that I have mentioned in chapter 6, or you can use the tool's guide depending on the pain.

Pay attention to your body's response and how it feels as you stretch and do each exercise. Once you have tried all the techniques, you will be able to identify which ones are best for you. Depending on your body's needs, such as shoulder pain, neck strain or low back tension, you can choose between one technique or one tool. Next, you can practice the stretching technique that is best for the area of pain and then use your body maintenance tool for 10 minutes each day. My clients may continue to work through the whole system to address all of their imbalances. Because the body is constantly changing, clients can modify the system by changing the tool and technique they use every day.

The system won't be complete in 10 minutes the first day. This is understandable. After you have mastered the skills and improved your ability to incorporate the system into your daily life, 10 minutes will be a manageable and sustainable time frame to continue using the system every day. You will be able to maintain your pain-free posture by your skills, abilities, and consistency in applying the system daily.

The 10-Minute Body Maintenance Program is now a new habit:

- *that you do at least once a day*
- *that takes you only 10 minutes*
- *Once you have the knowledge, it is easy to make this a reality.*

You can practice mindful breathing as you go through each technique. Pay attention to how your body feels as you breathe in and exhale.

Let's get started!

Neck Stretch

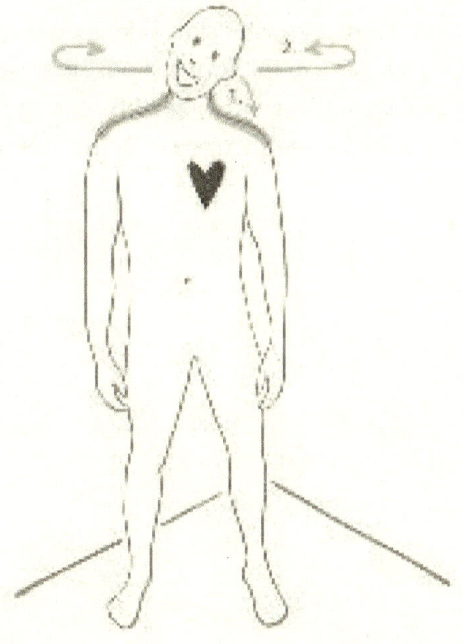

Neck Stretch

This stretch will not only be felt in your neck, but also in other areas of your neck. You may feel a stretching sensation or release from your neck to your shoulders and up your upper back. This is normal.

1. Take six deep breaths while looking down at your neck. Repeat the process on the opposite side.Take six deep, focused breaths and place your neck in the forward position. Repeat the process on the opposite side.Take six deep breaths and look down at your neck. Switch sides and repeat.Be curious. Breathe in and notice?

Upper Body Nerve Glide

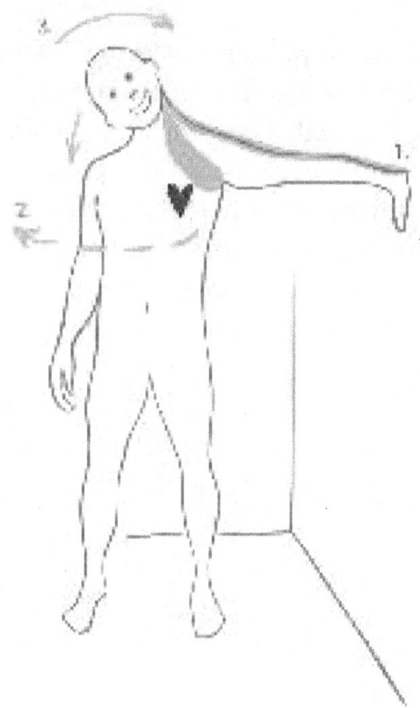

Upper Body Nerve Glide

This simple exercise will bring your neck, arm and wrist, wrist, hand, as well as your fingertips, alive. Do not avoid sharp pain near the edge of your comfort zone. Instead, embrace the intense stretch that may feel from your neck down to your forearm and fingers. As you glide the nerve through your entire arm, it is normal to feel intense stretching.

1. Arm: Gently press your right palm against the wall using your fingers. Gently extend your elbow.Maintain your arm position, but rotate your body away from the wall.Neck: Turn your head toward the left shoulder, and tilt your ear towards the left. Repeat 10 times. Do not hold the stretch, but instead gently move from the tilted to neutral position 10 times. Repeat the steps on the opposite side (left-hand side against the wall).Be curious. Take a deep breath and observe?

Chest Opener

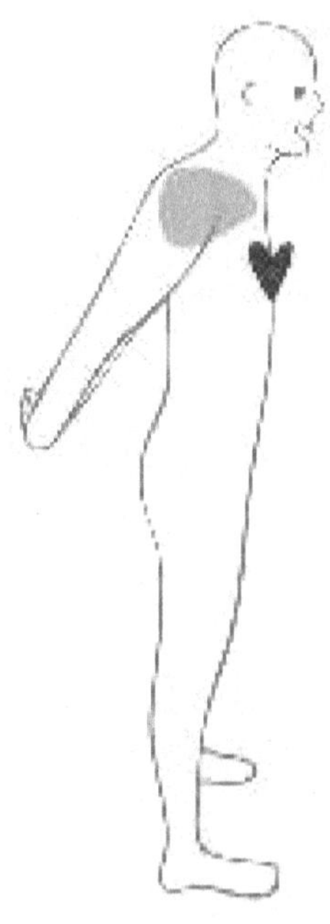

Chest Opener Stretch

This chest opener will cause a chain reaction of sensations that runs from your neck to your upper arm to your forearm to your hand.

1. Hold your hands together behind you.Arms: Lift your hands from your low back and hold it for six deep breaths.Be curious. Take a deep breath and observe?

Shoulder Reset Stretch

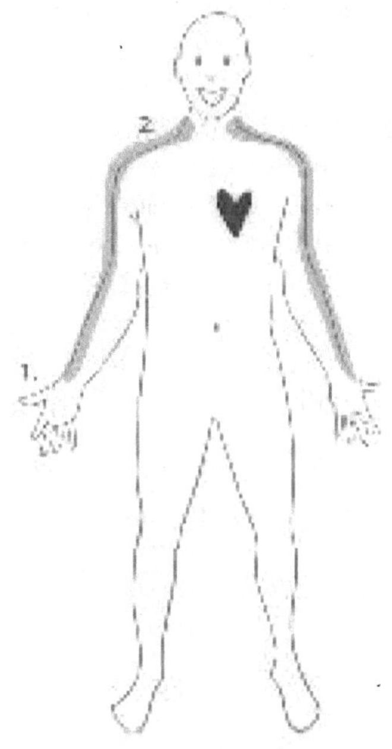

Shoulder Reset Stretch

This stretch activates a group of muscles that haven't been used often by people with Upper Crossed Syndrome or prolonged sitting. Your upper back muscles will also be engaged by allowing your chest to expand fully.

Sometimes fatigue can build up in your back muscles from holding the stretch. This is normal, it's actually a good thing. Accept it and breathe in it.

1. Your body: Stand with your palms slightly in front of your body with your hands reaching towards the ground with your chin tucked.Your shoulder blades: Gently squeeze your shoulders down and backward. Keep your chin down and take six deep breaths.Be curious. Take a deep breath and observe?

Shoulders + Mid Back Stretch

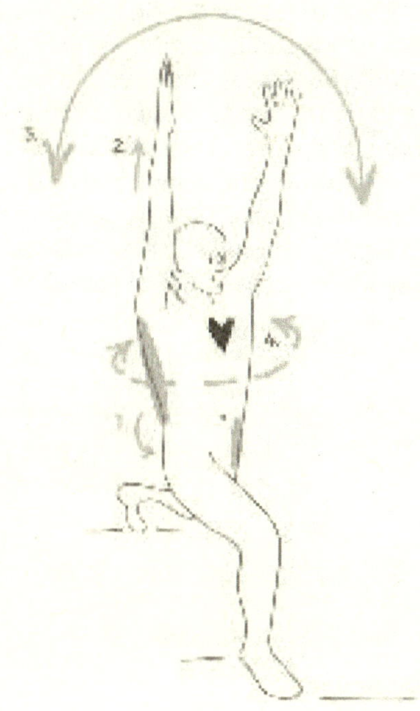

Shoulders + Mid Back Stretch

This exercise is likely to be the most difficult. Slowly, carefully, and with a lot of intention, move into this exercise. This exercise activates the whole body, not just its parts.

1. Body: assume lunge position, trunk upright, core engaged,tailbone tucked under.Reach your hands up toward the sky with your hands and hold it for six breaths. Relax your shoulders.With your hands above your head, bend your elbows to the left and right sides as though your upper body were between two glass planes. Take six deep breaths each side.Reach your hands out to your chest and turn your body until you feel tension in both directions. Take six deep breaths each side.Legs: Now switch legs and do the same exercise on each side.Be curious. Take a deep breath and observe?

Seated Spine Stretch

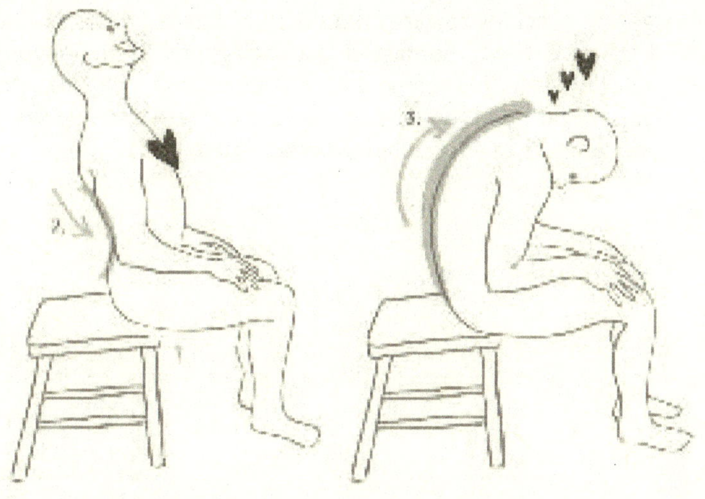

Seated Spine Stretch

Do not be alarmed if you hear a "snap crackle, pop" as you stretch. This is your spine and muscles relaxing and resetting themselves as they move through a wider range of motion. Regularly reset your spine, whether you are sitting at your desk or on a plane.

1. Body: Sit on the edge and place your hands on your thighs.Hips: Inhale and tilt your pelvis forward. Next, arch your lowback gently, reaching towards the sky.Hips: Inhale and tilt your pelvis backward. Next, round your low back gently. Then, let your head relax towards your chest.Follow your curiosity: Pay attention to your breath and repeat six times the forward and backward movements of your pelvis. How do you feel?

Piriformis Stretch

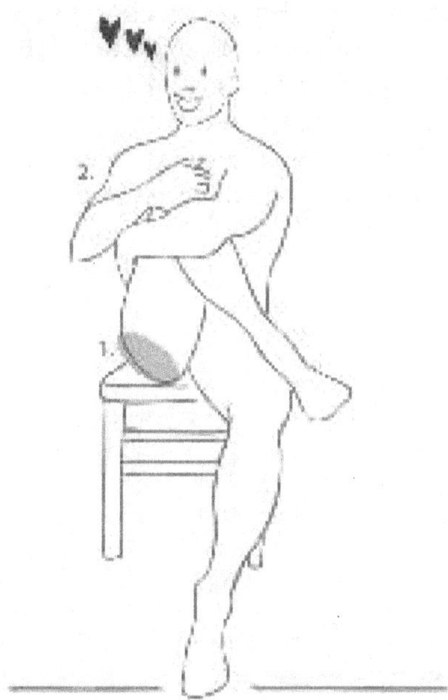

Piriformis Stretch

Make your hips come alive with this oh-so-good, deep posterior hip stretch. By lengthening bound-up hip muscles, this exercise releases persistent pulling in the low back and hip after prolonged sitting.

1. Body: sit on the edge of your chair and place one ankle on youropposite thigh or shin. Stay tall in your trunk.
2. Hips: maintain "neutral pelvis" and hug your knee toward theopposite shoulder. Hold for six breaths. Switch to the other side and repeat with your other knee. NOTE: If you feel pinching in the hip that you are hugging, release your hug to avoid pinching the soft tissue in your hip.
3. Be curious: gently twist your spine toward the knee you arehugging. Breathe and notice; what do you feel and where?

Hamstring + Low Back Stretch

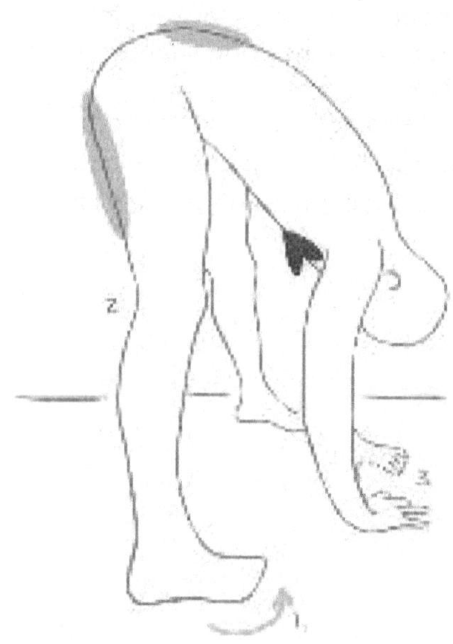

Hamstring + Low Back Stretch

This stretch uses self-created traction to bring a cascade of relief from the outer hips down through your legs and into your toes. Meanwhile, the back, neck, and spine are unloaded by using your own body weight. This stretching technique is natural, gentle traction at its best!

1. Feet: spread your feet a little wider than hip-width apart. Turnyour toes inward.
2. Body: from an upright stance position, walk your hands downyour body, creating a forward fold from your hips. If your hands do not reach the floor, support your trunk with your hands on your shins.
3. Legs: gently straighten both your knees and hold for six breaths.
4. Be curious: reach your hands to the outside of both of your feet. Breathe and notice; what do you feel and where?

Hip + Quad Stretch

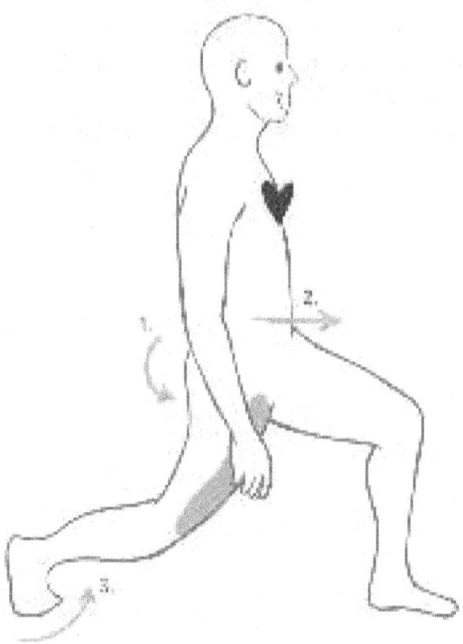

Hip + Quad Stretch

Be sure to maintain your upper body alignment as you step into this challenging stretch, which targets the front of the hip, inner thigh, lower leg, and low back muscles. With just a little rotation of the foot inward, you'll elongate the tight muscles at the front of your hip.

1. Body: assume lunge position, core engaged, trunk upright,tailbone tucked under.
2. Hips: square your hips so they are both facing forward.
3. Back foot: turn your toes inward and hold for six breaths. Switchto the other side and repeat.
4. Be curious: tilt your pelvis forward and backward to find your "neutral pelvis." Breathe and notice; what do you feel and where?

Calf + Lower Leg Stretch

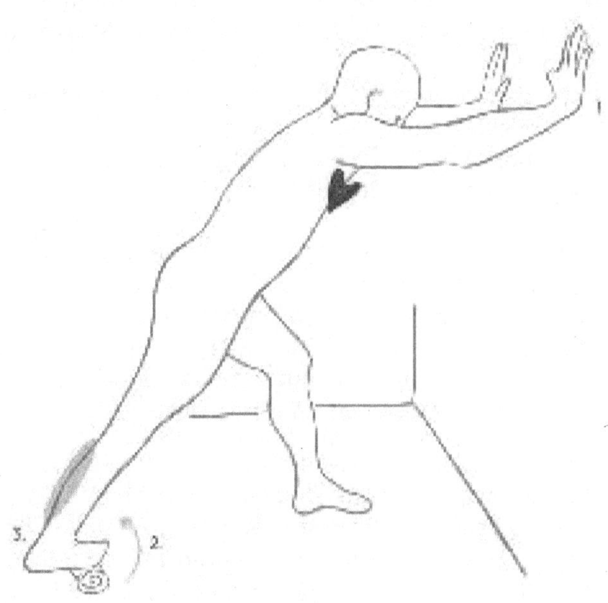

Calf + Lower Leg Stretch

Not everyone thinks to stretch out the calf and lower leg to relieve spine and body strain. Allow this exercise to reengage those oft-ignored muscles. You'll wake up a number of tight muscles, lengthening them from right behind and around the knee, down into your calf, and around your foot.

1. Body: facing a wall, step into a lunge position, with your handstouching the wall.
2. Back leg: put the ball of your foot on an approximately three-inchtowel roll with your toes turned inward. A hand towel works great.
3. Back leg: push your heel into the ground and hold for six breaths.Switch to the other side and repeat.
4. Be curious: breathe as you turn your toes slightly more inward.What do you feel and where?

You did it! By learning and applying these 10 stretching techniques, you have a daily system for head-to-toe body maintenance. With each of these stretching techniques, remember that practice makes progress. It's not about permanence or perfection. With just 10 minutes a day of taking action and practicing these stretching techniques, you can create a new habit and make this system part of your active, pain-free lifestyle.

At minimum, you are now aware that body maintenance is critical to achieving the sensations, body state, and feelings you desire (Part I). And you now have a practical, specific prescription—the 10-Minute Body Maintenance System—to live pain-free, energized, and confident. Now I challenge you to make this system a routine part of your workday so that you can truly achieve and live your desired results and outcomes!

PART III Results & Outcomes

"Success is no accident. It is hard work, perseverance, learning, studying, sacrifice, and most of all, love of what you are doing or learning to do." —Pelé

Now you know the tools, techniques, and strategies to live and sustain your pain-free life. Yet do you find you're struggling to make it all part of your day-to-day life? Does it all feel difficult because of limited time, money, or other barriers that are discouraging you from achieving your goals? What exactly is getting in your way?

I'm willing to guess that some of you are struggling with daily, consistent application of your new knowledge and skills. When other people tell me about their resistance, I hear statements like:

I don't have time.
I'm too busy.
It's impossible for me to do it alone.
I don't have the energy.
I am afraid I will make my pain worse.
I don't have the support I need.
I don't have enough money.
I don't know where to start.

Do any of these common statements sound familiar to you? At times, we all try to justify why we cannot make a change.

From my own experience, I have always found the resources necessary to support my desires. Don't get me wrong. I catch myself making plenty of excuses. I have even created deliberate routines with clear cues to remind myself of my vision and how I want to live my pain-free life. And sometimes I still struggle, coming up with some excuse or another.

However, here's the reality: Making excuses is a bad habit. So, I coursecorrect, focusing on my goals that align with my lifelong vision. And then it's about taking little steps and giving my best effort.

And so, too, can you do this. Replace the excuse making with a good habit, one that moves you from pain to possibility. The key to navigating bumps in the road and working around roadblocks is all about reconnecting to your vision.

Chapter 8: Act with Accountability to Sustain Momentum

"Set a goal, and in small, consistent steps, work to reach it. Get support from your peers when you start flagging. Repeat. You will change."
—Seth Godin

Many people say that adopting habits to create a healthier lifestyle affects different aspects of their life. When they make decisions that align with their vision, their actions produce a growing sense of purpose and vitality. They become more aware of their intuition. They gain clarity and confidence in their purpose, which drives greater self-initiative. They feel invigorated with newfound knowledge and abilities to manage their pain independently. Ultimately, this is all about transformation—even freedom. Instead of feeling pain, they realize they're focused on possibility. Their pain isn't *pushing* them. Their possibility is *pulling* them.

You can find your freedom by becoming your own guide. Own your ability (and responsibility) to move toward your goals. Yet even with this sense of ownership, having accountability will be essential to your success.

In helping people achieve their goals, I've noticed that having a buddy is the best way for them to remain accountable. So, if you are struggling with commitment, you may benefit from the support of an accountability partner or even a group.

For example, consider working with a physical therapist, yoga therapist, personal trainer, athletic trainer, or health coach. But if for any reason this option isn't for you, or if you don't want to ask a friend or colleague to help you, don't beat yourself up about it. Consider a membership at a yoga studio, join the local sports club, or sign up for seasonal intramural groups. After all, people are hardwired for connection. With a group, the connection, community, and unity toward a common goal create belief—namely, the belief that you can accomplish your goals. This is the power of groups and shared experiences.

Tracking Your Health Progress

It's also important to track your progress toward your goals. As your guide, I've developed a Healthy Habit Tool that you can start using immediately.

Keep this tracking tool handy so you can conveniently monitor your progress.
Simply mark a "Y" or "N" in each box if you have completed the 10-Minute Body Maintenance System for the day. You can also use it to track other goals, such as standing for three hours during your workday. Then mark a happy, neutral, or sad smiley face depending on how you felt that day while

working toward your goal. (See Appendix B for a version you can copy and use.)

Healthy Habit Tool

Goal: 10 Minute Body Maintenance

Motion Therapy	Week 1	[illegible]	[illegible]	[illegible]	[illegible]	[illegible]	[illegible]	[illegible]	[illegible]	[illegible]
[illegible]										
[illegible]										
[illegible]										
Thursday										
Friday										
Saturday										
Sunday										
[illegible]										
[illegible]										

If you prefer tracking your progress in another way, that's perfectly fine. You can journal, use an app on your smartphone (such as Way of Life, Momentum, and My Habits, or invest in a wearable fitness tracker to create accountability. The point is to do something! Take action.

Finally, you can also boost your odds of success through ***self-pacing and graded exposure***. These are perhaps best discussed in *Explain Pain*, a neuroscience and pain education book I love to reference when working with clients. In the chapter entitled "Pacing and Graded Exposure," the authors outline five ways to pace yourself effectively.[22] Below, I've summarized the steps and adapted them to the context here:

1. **Choose what you'll do more.** Pick a specific activity that's challenging for you, like standing at your workstation for three hours per day, five days a week, over the next two weeks.

2. **Note your baseline.** How much of the activity you've chosen can you do without a flare-up, such as pain or some other symptom? Whatever you can "definitely" do without pain, symptoms, or feeling desperate, this is your baseline. Use it as your starting point, or what you'll build upon at first.

3. **Plan your progression.** The point is to make incremental improvements toward your goal while being patient with yourself. If you walked 15 minutes today without pain symptoms, you may try 17 minutes tomorrow, 19 minutes the next day, 21 minutes the day after that, etc. Plan ahead for this progressive, conscientious style of improvement, and it will feel more doable both mentally and physically. You'll be guaranteed to experience little wins along the way. Even just making the effort to create your plan can also provide you with a feeling of personal *wow*!

4. **Accept any flare-ups.** Pain is not the goal, so if you notice you're suddenly flaring up, it's your body's alarm telling you that enough is enough—for now. Pay attention to it. Honor that honest communication. Don't give up on the practice you've adopted, but scale back until you've recovered, then step it up a notch once again. Don't quit your activity—keep trying, and your body will eventually embrace this change.

5. **Make it your lifestyle.** No doubt, you'll have to plan your life a bit more, but the activities you're choosing to do, or the habits you're now adopting, will bring you joy, even if it's just small bursts of joy. Schedule these activities into what you're doing on a more regular basis. Invite friends and family members to join and support you when you can. These folks don't need to be your official accountability partners; ask anyone you like or love to join in on your fun! Over time, you'll come to believe this is simply who you are and what you do.

Whatever you do, make accountability and checking-in a habit that's convenient for you. Otherwise, you'll struggle. When you keep the momentum going over the long haul, you'll be more likely to sustain your active lifestyle habits.

Chapter 9: Embrace the 3Cs—Commitment, Convenience, and Consistency

"We are what we repeatedly do.
Excellence, then, is not an act but a habit."
—Aristotle

It never fails. When a client experiences a win with immediate relief, makes progress, and generates momentum toward living injury-free and pain-free, they often ask, "What do I need to do next?" Here's what I say:

Sustainable gains are achieved by practicing good habits.

Like many of my clients, you are creating new habits, and the choices, activities, and behaviors that you repeatedly practice become your lifestyle. There will be bumps in the road, even unforeseen roadblocks. If you want to feel better, however, you will need to dig deep for the willpower and strength to keep practicing the right habits. To do that with success requires relentless focus on what I call the "3Cs."

- You honor this process with **Commitment**
- You make your habits **Convenient**
- You practice them with **Consistency**

Marie Forleo, one of my online marketing mentors, regularly says, "Clarity comes through engagement, not thought."[23] So you have to take action and engage with your *commitments*, find ways to *conveniently* integrate the best practices into your daily living, and *consistently* move toward achieving your goals.

Here's a breakdown of the 3Cs:

COMMITMENT. This is about doing what you've promised yourself you will do. You've already created clarity around your vision and set goals. And, you've also committed to learning the Tools & Techniques that will empower you to achieve greater health, happiness, and performance. But sustaining your commitment requires that you reengage with it regularly. It requires staying inspired on a daily basis. Everybody's approach to this will be unique, but here are some activities I recommend for maintaining a daily commitment to your health and wellness vision:

- **Address what's working and what's not.** Pay close attention to when and how you've been successful relative to your goals. When you've come up short, what's going on? What steps can you take to address any obstacles so you're regularly committed to achieving what you want to feel—that possibility you desire and deserve?

- **Be intentional and deliberate.** Good intentions are meaningless if you don't take purposeful action. Use your SMART goals to take you in the direction of your health and wellness vision. Design your life, be intentional, and take deliberate action in your day-to-day activities.

- **Practice gratitude**. Be grateful for the health and wellness that you have at this moment. Yes, we can improve in some or many areas of our life. At the moment, you are breathing, reading, and reflecting on these strategies, and it is important to practice gratitude for where you are right now.

- **Practice visualization.** Use your mind's eye to imagine your active, healthy, vibrant self. Visualization is a powerful tool for allowing you to "see" your pain-free body, know your mindset, and feel your spirit, all free of dis-ease and full of life, energy, and self-confidence.

CONVENIENT. Let's face it—if something isn't convenient to do, then we're less likely to do it, period. So, it's essential to develop ways to make your habit realistic or practical to do. Here are some ideas for boosting the convenience factor:

- **Learn to use your excuses.** We often make excuses for why we aren't achieving our goals. Usually those excuses relate to the fact that it's inconvenient to do something, even though we know it will improve our ability to succeed. If you're making excuses, don't judge or criticize yourself for it. But do note and use them to take corrective action and address the issues. For example, if you are making a lot of excuses in regard to time, then that's your cue that you've got an activity-management issue you need to address

  if you're going to make progress toward your goal.

- **Check in on your alignment.** No matter where you are or what you're doing, you can easily self-assess your alignment and course-correct if you're off track. You can also take a photo of yourself at your desk or workstation. Using this visual image, quickly determine how you "stack up" in regard to the alignment techniques you've learned. Go back to the section with aligned standing and aligned sitting for a quick check.

- **Assess your active workstation.** Is it working? For example, is your exercise ball collecting dust in a nearby closet? Switch out your chair for the ball instead. If you're finding you're not using your workstation because there are some issues with the height, do the necessary remodeling or grab a stack of books to lift up your monitor to eye level. (See five steps in chapter 6 for aligned sitting and standing.) The point is to do it all correctly so using these tools becomes easier and more convenient than not using them.

- **Invest in an active workstation.** Wanting to upgrade from a DIY version of your active workstation to something that perhaps has more style, functionality, or flexibility? You're in luck. Go to my website (motiontherapy.net) to access additional resources.

- **"Plant" tools in familiar places.** For example, you can purchase an active seat, put it in your living room, and use it when you watch your favorite shows. Or as we discussed earlier, you can do things like deliberately place your foam roller on the bedroom floor so it becomes incorporated into your nightly routine. If you've got a Thera Cane, you can also put it in your car's middle console so it's easy to grab and use after a long drive. It's easy enough to place a spiky ball in your shower. Using it to give yourself a mini massage will become the "excuse" you need to spend that extra five minutes under the hot water.

CONSISTENCY. In addition to commitment and convenience, being consistent with your mindset and behaviors is a vital key to achieving your goals. In a podcast interview featured in Lewis Howes's *The School of Greatness*, John Maxwell states, "Consistency will give you a compounding that no other trait will." Like compound interest, its exponential growth leads to significant gains.[24]

Here are a few ways to improve consistency:

- **Use reminders and/or cues.** Starting new practices and changing up a routine can be tough. But if you simply get started, you'll find you're much more motivated to follow through. The trick is to figure out ways to trigger your new, good habits, such as:

✓ Through your active workstation of choice, for example, the standing desk plus a yoga/exercise ball for your seated desk and a spiky ball on the surface of your workstation. Even something as simple as sticky notes with reminders to move on the half-hour can help.

✓ With active lifestyle technology by trying your favorite apps. Consider those like UpDesk and Stand Up!, for example. Or you might check out resources like juststand.org and give wearable tools like a fitness tracker, iWatch, or Lumo Lift a try.

✓ By practicing greater body awareness, to acknowledge and listen to your body. Practice being present with your body's sensations. What are they telling you? To hydrate? Move? Take a break? Do it!

- **Implement an accountability system.** Designing your accountability plan is a great first step. But then you've got to implement it. Take that critical action!

- **Schedule a "progress report,"** ideally every 14 days, to reflect, self-check, and measure your progress toward your SMART goals. You can also plan a weekly, monthly, or quarterly meeting with your mentor, coach, or accountability partner to maintain your momentum toward your goals. Progress reports are a proven method for consistently tracking your success. You can place a reminder on your smartphone to check the app, fitness tracker, Healthy Habit Tool, etc. that includes your SMART goals.

- **Strengthen your NO "muscle."** When you're feeling tempted by others to do something that takes you off course from your goals, have a comeback ready that's easy to remember. This will take you to newer, better places as you learn to prioritize your life and create the resources (time, money, energy, etc.) to do what's best for you. Once you're on board, you'll find you've got more resources to do what you know feels right. Eventually, these new strategies will be easier to implement and manage.

- **Plan ahead.** As the saying goes, "Failing to plan is planning to fail." So, create a regular plan for how you'll build more motion into your life. Write it down so it's in black and white. Schedule the 10-Minute Body Maintenance System in your calendar just as you would a very important appointment. Make it as much a nonnegotiable as your shower or morning coffee. Then put things in place that will help keep you on track.

These suggestions are just a few of many ways you can remain more committed to achieving your vision, make the Tools & Techniques convenient so you will use them, and become more consistent in your daily practices. With this foundation, you can learn how to create the habits that will support your active, pain-free lifestyle.

Chapter 10: Create Habits That Support Your Active Lifestyle

"It's never too late to redefine self-control, to change long ingrained habits, and to do the work you're capable of."
—Seth Godin

You now know how focusing on the 3Cs can support the habits you'll need to master. But how do you actually create those good habits required to support your pain-free lifestyle? Knowledge is power, and I've found it helpful to dig deeper into the psychology and biology of behavior change and habits in general. So, let's explore what habits are, how they form, and how to create new ones to support our active lifestyle.

The Truth About Habits.

Habits are learned mindsets or activities that, over time, require little to no effort by our bodies and our brains. A habit is a behavior you do without thinking; it should be more or less automatic.

In forming new habits, the simplest place to start is focusing on new behaviors or routines you actually *want to do*. If a particular new behavior or routine feels like a "should"—something you're forced to do—it probably will not become a true habit. So, when you're learning how to create a new habit, don't focus on the obligation; instead, focus on the core desired feelings you intentionally want to create (defined in Part I).

Creating a new habit is the cornerstone to your success as you take action and apply everything you've been given in this guidebook. The goal is to adopt new, healthy habits that will enable you to achieve your goals. But if you don't know how to create those habits, you won't change.

One of the best ways to understand how habits are created comes from author Charles Duhigg in his book *The Power of Habit*. Using science-based research, Duhigg concludes that habits form through a "feedback loop." The feedback loop includes three elements:

> - first, the ***cue*** that kickstarts thinking or acting automatically; - then, some physical and/or emotional ***routine*** (something you do that may or may not be automatic);
> - and finally, the ***reward*** that tells your brain whether it's worth remembering the next time you're facing that familiar cue. If the reward is worth remembering, then the likelihood of a habit developing goes up. In essence, habits get set as that reward gets higher or feels better.[25] According to Duhigg:

"The reason the discovery of the habit loop is so important is that it reveals a basic truth: When a habit emerges, the brain stops fully participating in decision making. It stops working so hard, or diverts focus to other tasks. So unless you deliberately *fight* a habit—unless you find new routines—the pattern will unfold automatically."

Think about the habit loop this way: Can you identify with a midday slump and the desire to have a sugary treat? If you are not aware of the cue-routinereward feedback loop, then the routine of an occasional midday sweet can turn into a bad habit. If we can interrupt and change this routine, however, we can create a new habit.

The same goes for the 10-Minute Body Maintenance System. I regularly work with people who have a hard time being consistent with the system and therefore have a hard time making it a habit. They are extremely committed to living pain-free; however, they struggle to make their efforts convenient (part of a *routine*) so they can be consistent and form a new habit. By making the system part of their everyday routine, it can eventually become a habit that helps them achieve their pain-free vision.

The Feedback Loop

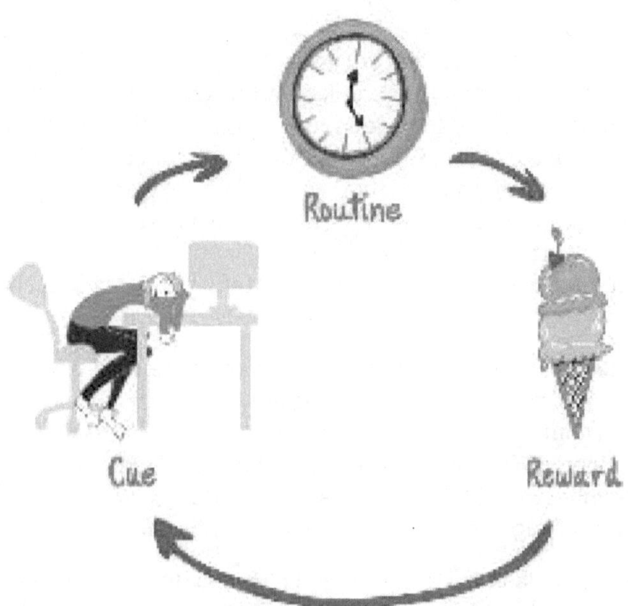

How Do I Create a New Habit?

There are a number of ways to create new habits based on the feedback loop:

1. Change the cue
2. Change the routine
3. Change the reward

First, we can *change the cue*s that trigger habits. So, if you hang around negative people who trigger you to talk about negative things like your pain, try shifting your social circle to include new, positive, and forward-focused friends. I bet you will eventually talk and think more about possibility and less about pain. You can also surround yourself with other resources to reinforce your commitment—listen to podcasts while you exercise, read inspiring books, watch TED Talks when folding laundry, and start your day with gratitude practices. Adopt that more grateful mindset for each bit of progress you've made.

Second, you can change your habits by *changing the reward* you want. If you've determined that the feeling you desire (from Part I) is to feel comfortable in your own skin, then that reward becomes the key motivator for using the Tools & Techniques you learned in Part II. As you use these Tools & Techniques—and back them up with a focus on the 3Cs—you will make shifts away from the pain toward your possibility.

Third, habits are more likely to stick if you *change your routine*. If you shake up what you normally do between the cue and the reward, you'll be more likely to succeed. The key is to establish a new routine and then practice it until it becomes automatic. The more thinking you do about your routine (e.g., making excuses not to do it or questioning whether you should do it today), the more you increase the odds that you will not get the desired results. We are working toward creating automatic behaviors.

For example, if you leave your active workstation in an upright position, you'll come back to it the next morning with a visual, physical, and functional reminder or cue to stand. The same is true if you use an app, timer, or alarm clock as a reminder to move about, reset your posture, or take a movement break with the 10-Minute Body Maintenance System. You will feel more energized and ready to tackle your next task, thus creating momentum with each small success.

The Habit Loop

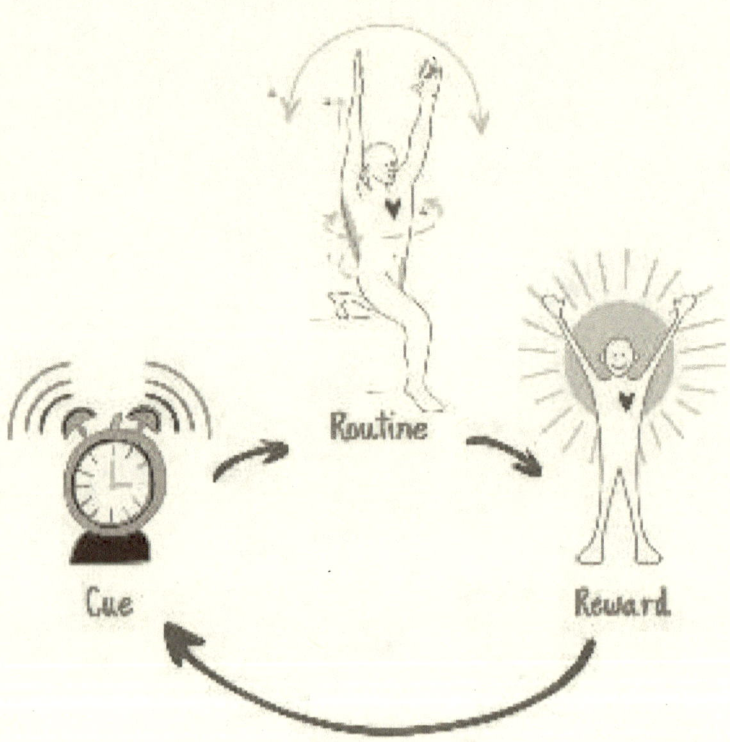

How Long Does a New Habit Take to Form?

Don't be surprised if it takes a long time to fully own these new habits. Perhaps you have heard the myth that it takes 21 days to form a habit. According to a study cited in *The British Journal of General Practice*,[26] "This myth appears to have originated from anecdotal evidence of patients who had received plastic surgery treatments and typically adjusted psychologically to their new appearance in twenty-one days." However, according to the current research, the sweet spot for forming a new habit is 66 days. I recommend giving yourself 10 weeks and understanding that forming a new habit is a process. Practice makes progress, not perfection or permanence. Some habits form quickly. Others may take a long, long time.

My experience in working with clients is that the knowledge, structure, and guidance to do the initial heavy lifting is missing when it comes to getting results and sustaining those results with healthy habits. People are reassured when I tell them that the first steps can be a lot less work if they focus on creating a new habit that actually rewards them with how they *want to feel*. Clients find that small successes build momentum, keep them motivated, and lead to more successes.

Without a doubt, people who ultimately reach their goals are those who are patient, persistent, and pace themselves as they journey through their individual process. They gain confidence with each small step taken to achieve goals that are aligned with their vision. They adopt the 3Cs and create new habits that enable them to live pain-free, energized, and confident.
In this way, they can truly live their life by design.

Conclusion

"Practice makes progress. Not perfection. Not permanence." —Heidi Roberts

This book isn't like most books where once you read it, you put it on a shelf or share it with a friend. Your journaling about your Pain & Possibility in Part I, learning the Tools & Techniques in Part II, and creating habits to achieve the Results & Outcomes in Part III are now very personal to you. They can be referred to and expanded upon time and time again as you continue on your health and wellness journey. Remember, practice makes progress. There is no such thing as perfection or permanence. Everything changes. So, in light of that . . .

Keep practicing. Remain curious. Stay consistent. Live pain-free by sustaining your active lifestyle at work, at home, and at play!

As you continue to take action, welcome new knowledge that will come to you. This book is just the beginning of understanding more about yourself as a growing individual. Over time, you'll come to discover what activities support you in feeling good and how those can consistently create the feelings you desire. Practicing these strategies, techniques, and tools will support a balanced body and how *you* want to *feel*.

Let this guidebook be part of the process for transforming pain, sustaining gains, and realizing your possibility. Remember, you must stay committed if you want to experience change. Your vision of success will become real only through your personal desire, discipline, and dedication.

Take advantage of the additional resources on my website. Join in on what is called "Motion Therapy," a world in which ambitious people manage their body imbalances to live pain-free. Keep trusting in yourself. Take one step at a time as you progress on your health and wellness journey. You can do it!

Acknowledgments

Thank you, my reader, for investing in this practical guidebook to support your health and wellness journey and transform your pain into your possibility while you work!

Thank you to my teachers, coaches, and mentors who have shared their wisdom through books, courses, podcasts, interviews, phone calls, walking meetings, and adventuring.

Thank you to my all-important community of family, friends, clients, and colleagues for listening, supporting, and encouraging me on my health and wellness journey.

A special thank you to the following people for being on this wild adventure with me:

To Mom and Dad-I am the woman I am today because of both of you.

To Eric Roberts and Teresa Roberts, I have learned from and been inspired by both of you and I have greater empathy, compassion, and grace because of you both in my life.

To Tim, you are the love of my life. I am a better person because of the love, patience, and dreams we've stepped into together.

To Katie Roberts, Julie Rocha Buel, Christina Roth, and Jennifer Stimson for bringing your hearts and talent to this project!

To my beta readers, thank you for believing in my mission and bringing your opinions and feedback to this project. My heartfelt gratitude for each of these beautiful women with whom I have been lucky enough to be on the planet at the same time: Erica Nelson, Lisa Hill, Shelli McClung, Lianro WagenerSmith, Gabrielle McGrew, Mary Stavrou, Juliet Maris, Theresa Perry, Eileen Garvin, Kristen Anne Campbell, and Jennifer Silapie.

Appendix A:

10-Minute Body Maintenance Exercises—Upper vs. Lower Body Techniques

10-Minute Body Maintenance
Upper Body Techniques

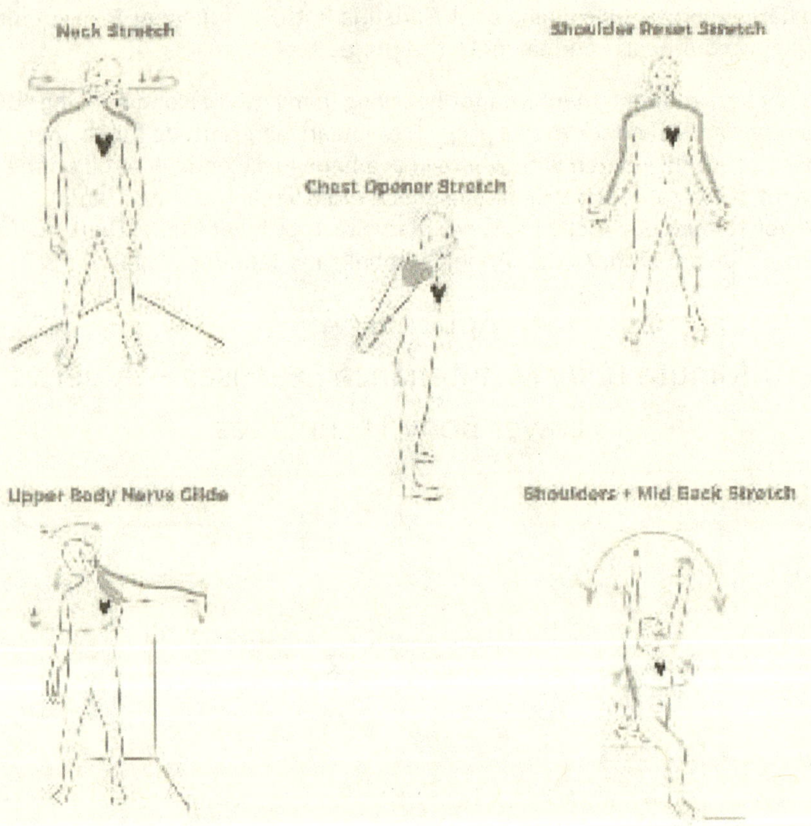

10-Minute Body Maintenance
Lower Body Techniques

Piriformis Stretch

Hamstring + Low Back Stretch

Hip + Quad Stretch

Seated Spine Stretch

Calf + Lower Leg Stretch

Appendix B: Healthy Habit Tool Chart

Healthy Habit Tool

Goal: 10 Minute Body Maintenance

[illegible]	Week 1	[illegible]	[illegible]	[illegible]	[illegible]	[illegible]	[illegible]	[illegible]	[illegible]	[illegible]
[illegible]										
[illegible]										
[illegible]										
Thursday										
Friday										
[illegible]										
[illegible]										
[illegible]										
[illegible]										

Notes

Glossary

Active workstation: a workspace designed to allow both aligned sitting and standing in order to optimize your body's performance. Commonly called "standing desks," "standing workstations," or "sit-stand workstations," active workstations enhance our mental, physical, and emotional health; support better digestion and overall body function; and can help lower the risk of Sitting Disease.

Aligned sitting: a technique designed to improve head-to-hip alignment and muscle engagement of the upper body; see also *aligned standing.*

Aligned standing: a technique designed to improve your standing alignment while engaging muscles of your entire body, specifically the pelvis, spine, shoulders, neck, upper back, and chin. Aligned standing assists you in moving properly as you remain active throughout the day. See also *aligned sitting.*

Alignment: the proper arrangement of all the body's muscles and bones. When all 640 muscles and 206 bones are in optimal alignment, your "system" is primed for optimal performance, and you can perform activities efficiently, effectively, and without pain or limitation. See also *posture.*

Body scan: a quick but powerful assessment tool for identifying pain in your body. Whether you're sitting still or standing still, it can help you notice what you are feeling, where you are feeling it, and how intense it is.

Cue: the first part of forming a habit according to the "feedback loop." The cue kickstarts thinking or acting automatically. See also *routine* and *reward.*

Goals: practical, attainable outcomes that you plan for and believe move you toward your vision. More than mere hopes or wishes, they are concrete stepping-stones that lead you down the path of a valued life. See also *shortterm goals* and *long-term goals*.

Habit: a behavior you do without thinking; a learned mindset or activity that, over time, requires little to no effort by our bodies and our brains. See also *practice* and *routine*.

Long-term goals: goals that become your ultimate reality, or part of your life.

Long-term goals may include lifelong habits such as incorporating the 10Minute Body Maintenance System into your daily practice. See also *shortterm goals*.

Lower Crossed Syndrome: muscular imbalances focused in the lower part of the body that are caused by poor posture and alignment. The source of imbalance is in opposing groups of tight muscles and weak muscles. See also *Upper Crossed Syndrome.*

Mindful breathing: proactively engaging your breathing muscles in a natural, balanced way while you breathe. Mindful breathing contributes to good alignment and enables greater mobility. It also provides the added benefit of calming the heart, mind, and body as a whole, highly integrated system; it enables greater patience for where you're at, what you notice, and what you feel. See also *mindfulness*.

Mindfulness: exercises or techniques aimed to increase awareness of the body, mind, and/or spirit and to improve focus on the task at hand. For the purposes of this book, mindfulness includes mindful breathing with the balloon breathing technique, *body scans*, and routine body work, such as the stretching exercises included in the 10-Minute Body Maintenance System. These practices ultimately help us make better choices in our journey of health and wellness. See also *mindful breathing*.

Nerve gliding: muscle stretches that help soft tissue move properly and therefore prevent related pain. Nerve gliding is aided by the body maintenance tools mentioned in this book, specifically the Stretch Out Strap and foam roller.

Posture: a snapshot of how you hold your body at any given moment. Proper posture is an outward sign that your body is accurately aligned. Posture is about what's seen, while alignment is about what's connected. See also *alignment.*

Practice: repeated exercise in or performance of an activity or skill so as to acquire and maintain proficiency in it. See also *habit* and *routine*.

Reward: the third part of forming a habit according to the "feedback loop." If your brain thinks a reward is worth remembering, then the likelihood of a habit developing increases. See also *cue* and *routine*.

Routine: something (physical and/or emotional) you do often that may or may not be automatic; the second part of forming a habit according to the "feedback loop." Healthy, consistent routines can help create good habits, such as practicing the 10-Minute Body Maintenance System every day. See also *habit* and *practice; cue* and *reward*.

Self-pacing and graded exposure: part of a step-by-step plan, described in depth in *Explain Pain*, that can boost the odds of success in accomplishing goals; steps include choosing what to do more, noting your baseline, planning your progression, accepting flare-ups, and making it your lifestyle.

Shift: a change in awareness of a sensation (e.g., relief, release, or greater mobility) that gets you closer to how you want to feel in your body. The exercises throughout this book help generate a shift toward your pain-free possibility.

Short-term goals: goals that equate to small successes and create momentum as you achieve them. Short-term goals are made based on what you want to accomplish and how you want to feel now. They support your *long-term goals* and ultimately, your *vision*.

Sitting Disease: the state of physical, mental, or emotional pain that results from having a sedentary lifestyle. The symptoms include everything from neck and back pain to depression, obesity, heart disease, and even cancer. Sitting Disease leads to acute and chronic health care conditions and is a contributing factor to *Lower Crossed Syndrome* and *Upper Crossed Syndrome.*

SMART goals: long-term and short-term goals that are **S**pecific, **M**easurable, **A**ttainable, **R**ealistic, and **T**ime-bound. Setting goals with each of these five attributes improves your success in achieving them. See also *long-term goals* and *short-term goals*.

Soft tissue: includes tendons, ligaments, fascia, skin, synovial membranes, muscles, nerves, and blood vessels. Proper and regular movement of the soft tissue helps prevent pain.

Trigger point: a sensitive area of the body that gets so irritated that the body misinterprets the pain signal, causing the person to feel as if the pain is coming from somewhere else. The five body maintenance tools and exercises mentioned in this book can help release trigger points.

Upper Crossed Syndrome: muscular imbalances in the upper body caused by poor posture and alignment. The source of imbalance is in the opposing group of tight muscles and weak muscles. See also *Lower Crossed Syndrome.*

Vision: the big, broad goal in your life. Your vision is the exciting picture of your future, your ultimate destination. It determines why you need to do—or not do—what you're doing. Your vision should be purposely crafted to motivate and inspire you to live an energized, confident, and pain-free life. See also *goals*.

www.ingramcontent.com/pod-product-compliance
Lightning Source LLC
LaVergne TN
LVHW041115150826
845673LV00007B/2059

* 9 7 9 8 7 7 5 7 6 1 4 2 4 *